# Relaxing Sce[illegible] Coloring Book: A Journey of Mindfulness with Stress and Anxiety Relief

*Carmela Crayon*


ISBN: 978-1-961909-08-3

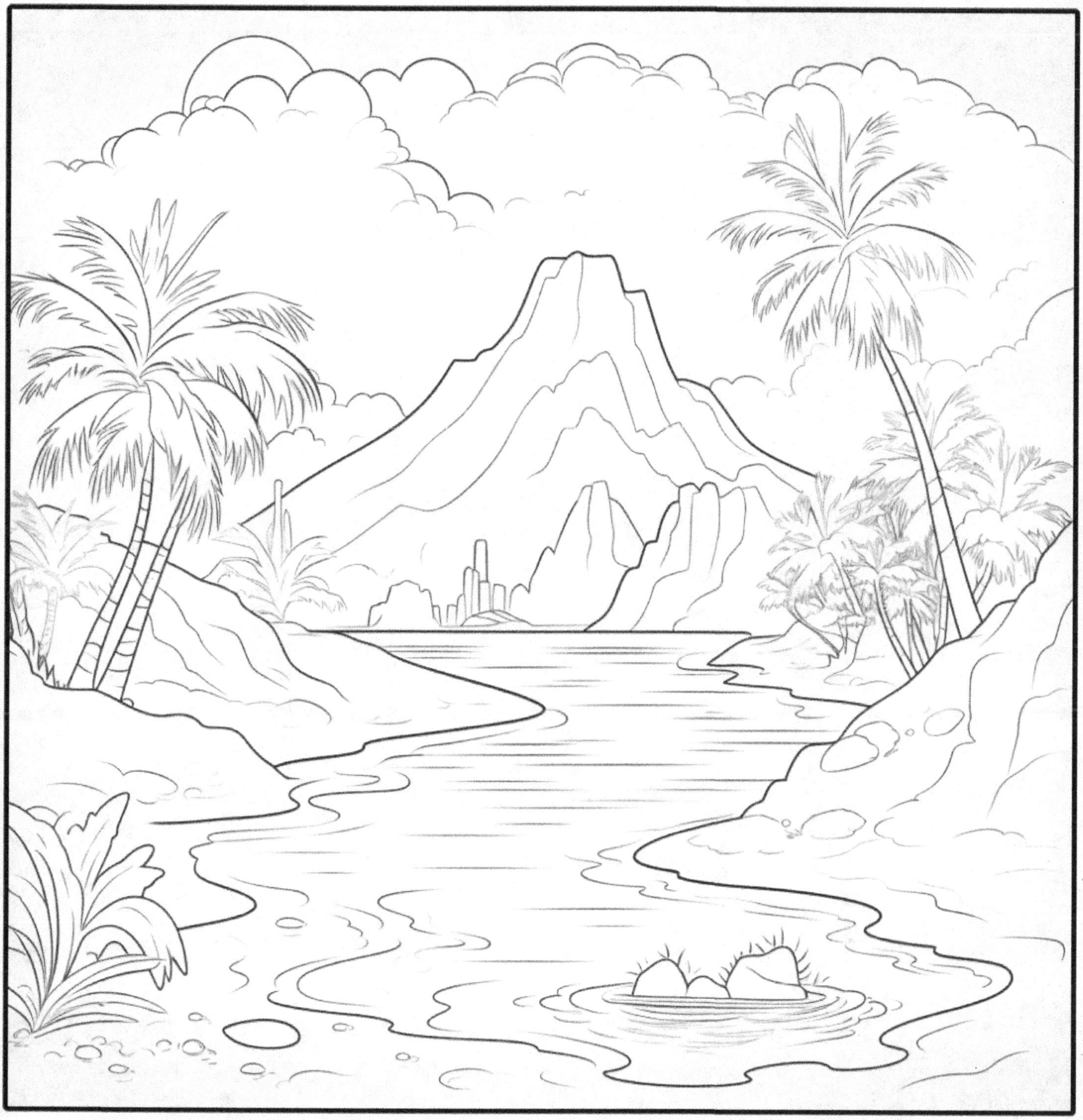

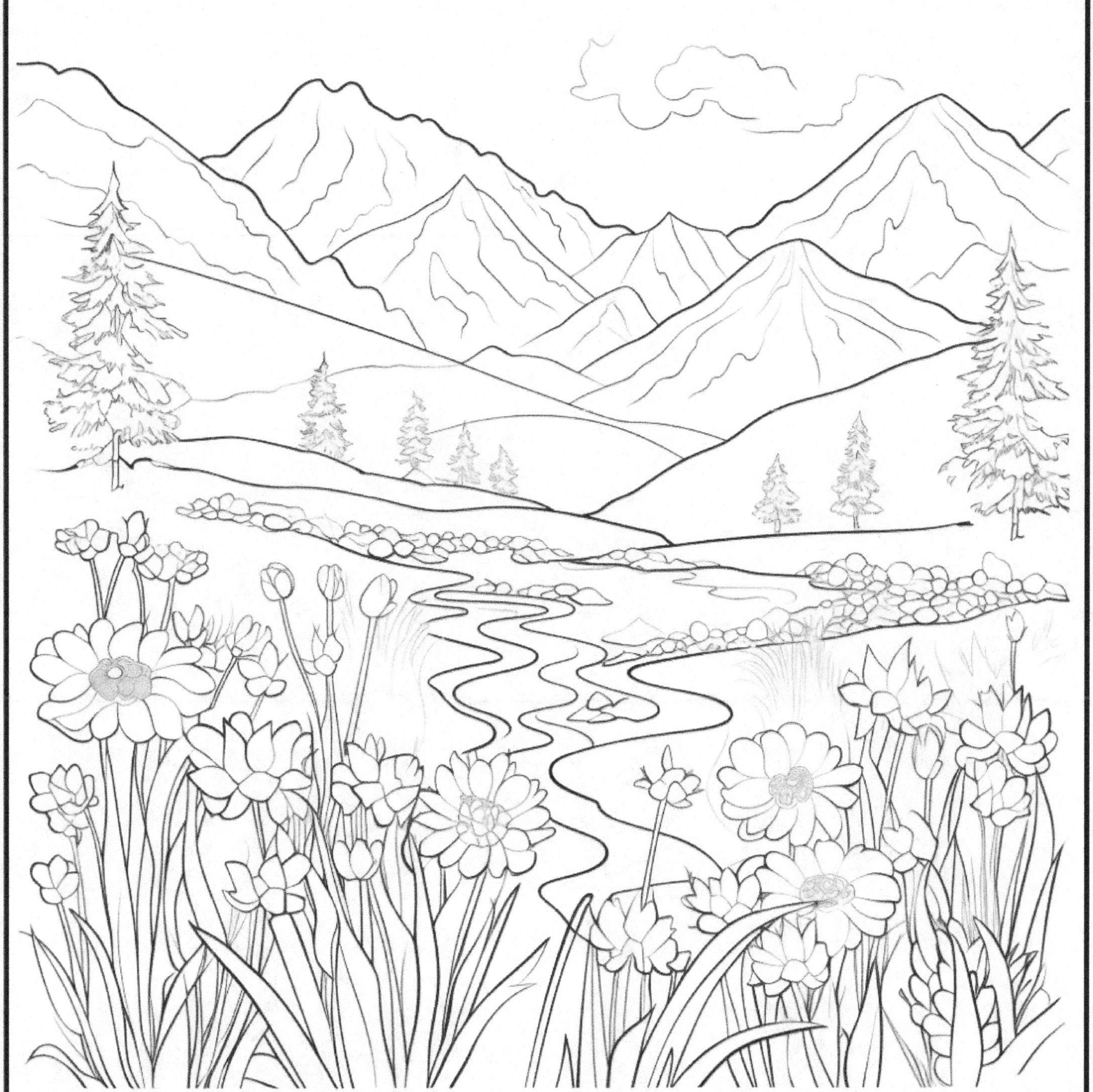

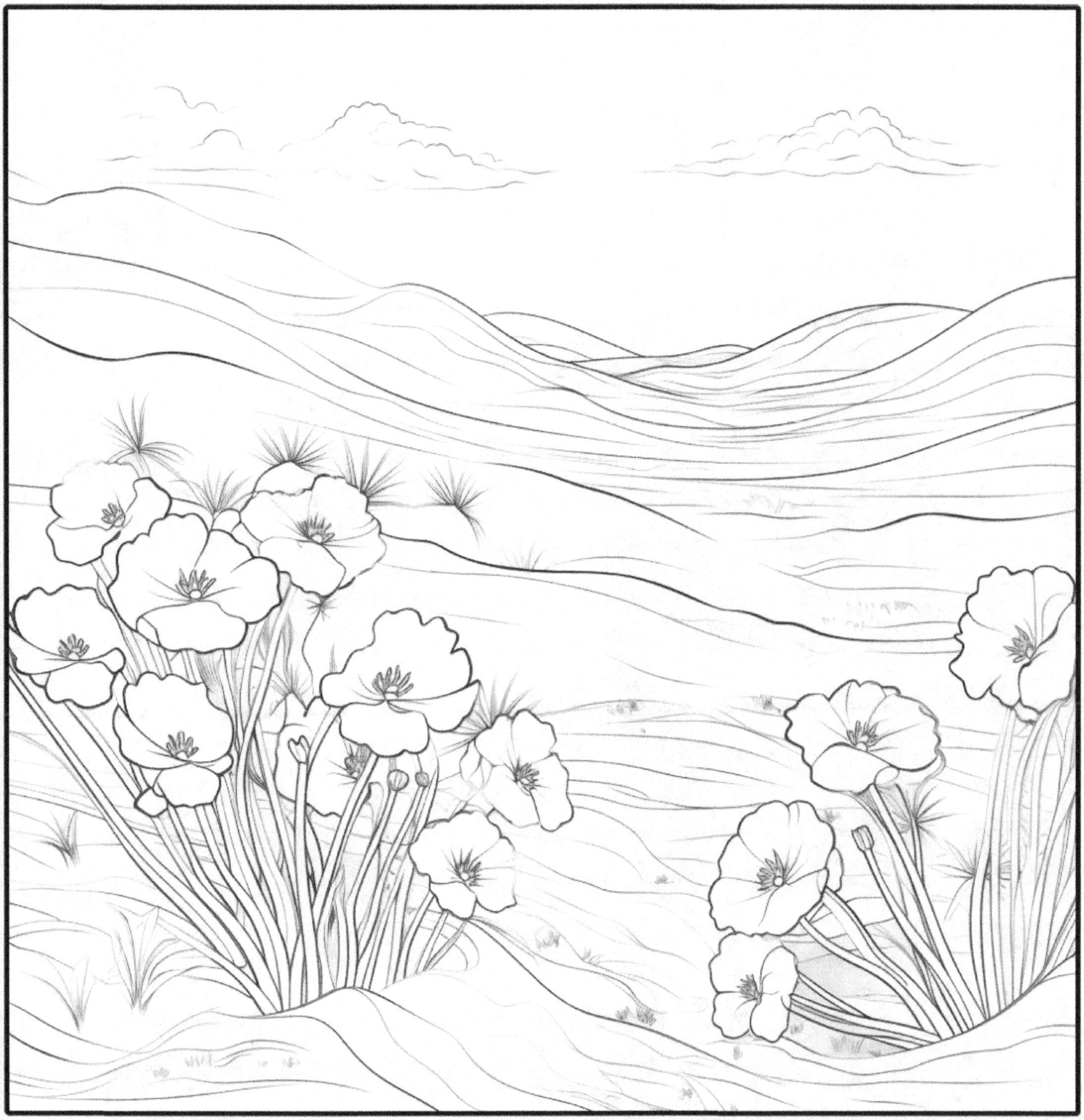

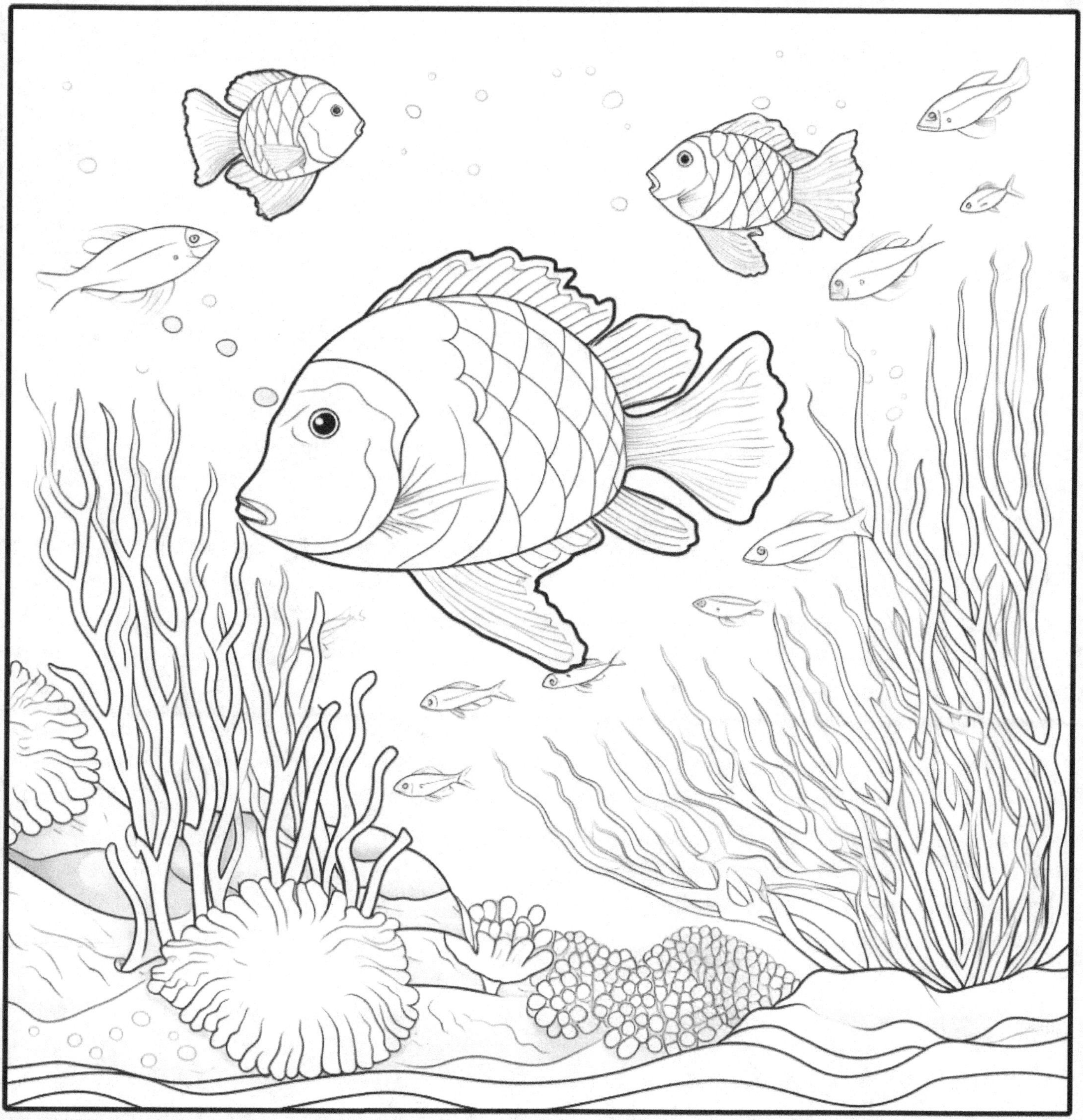

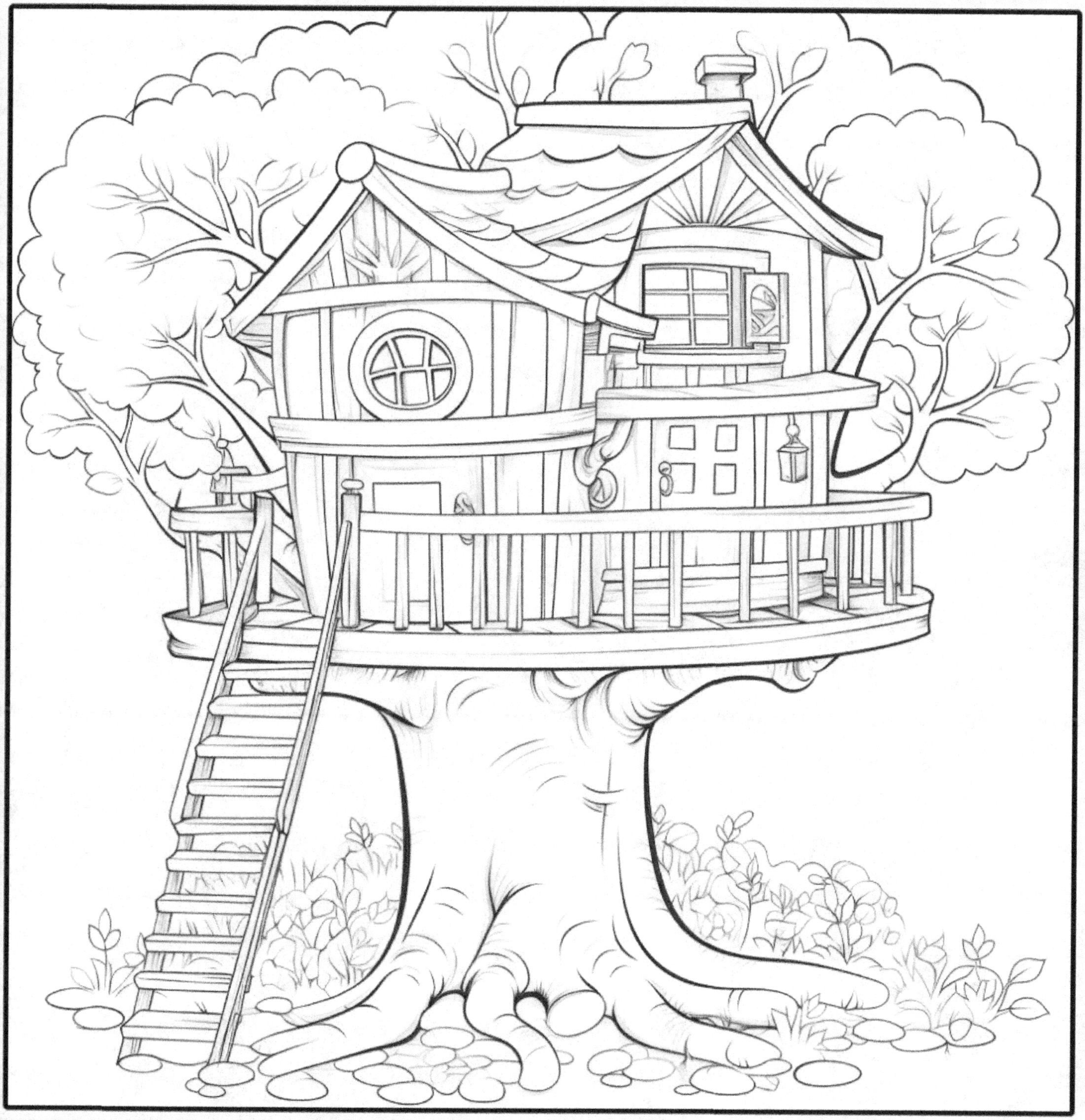

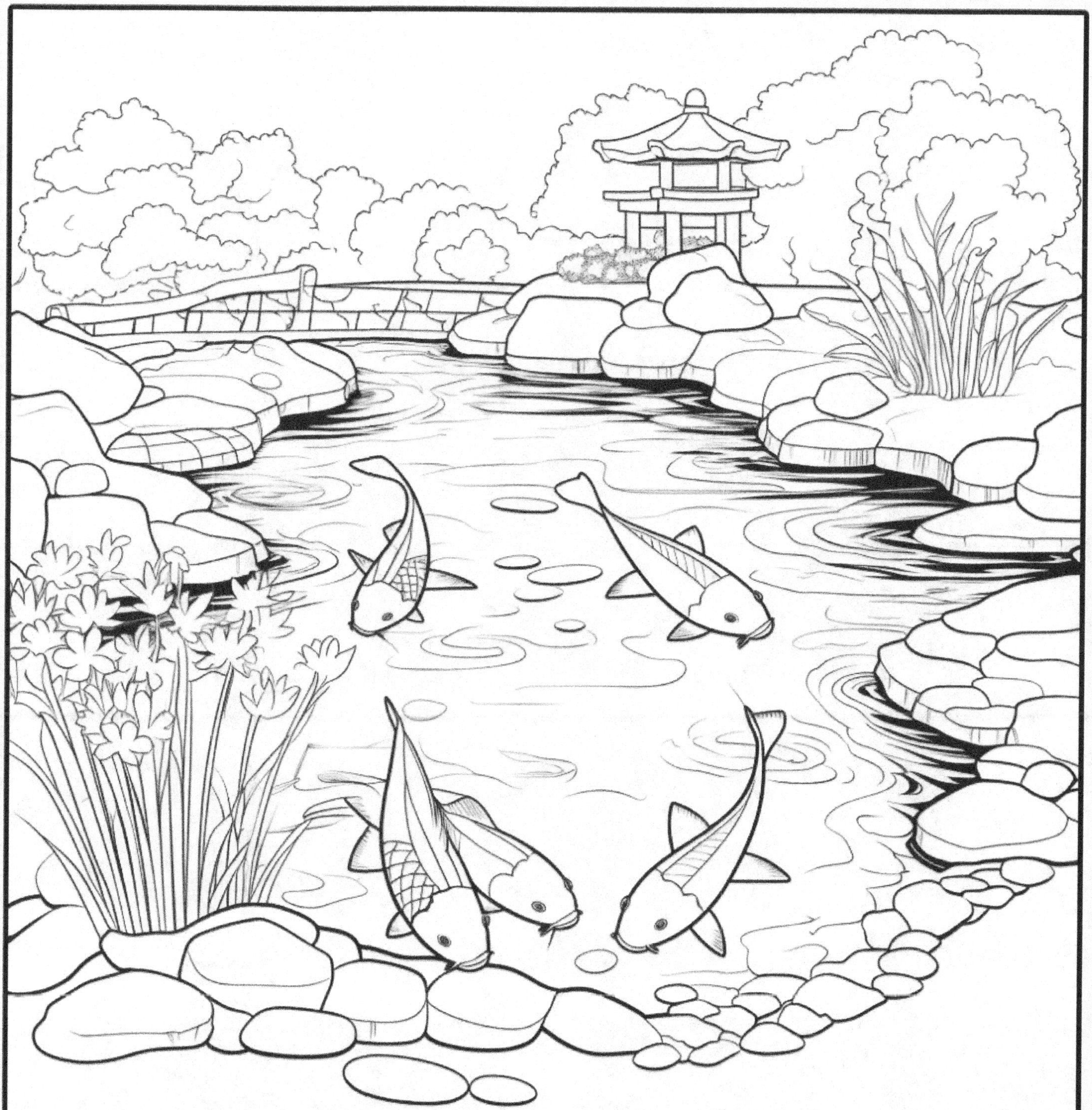

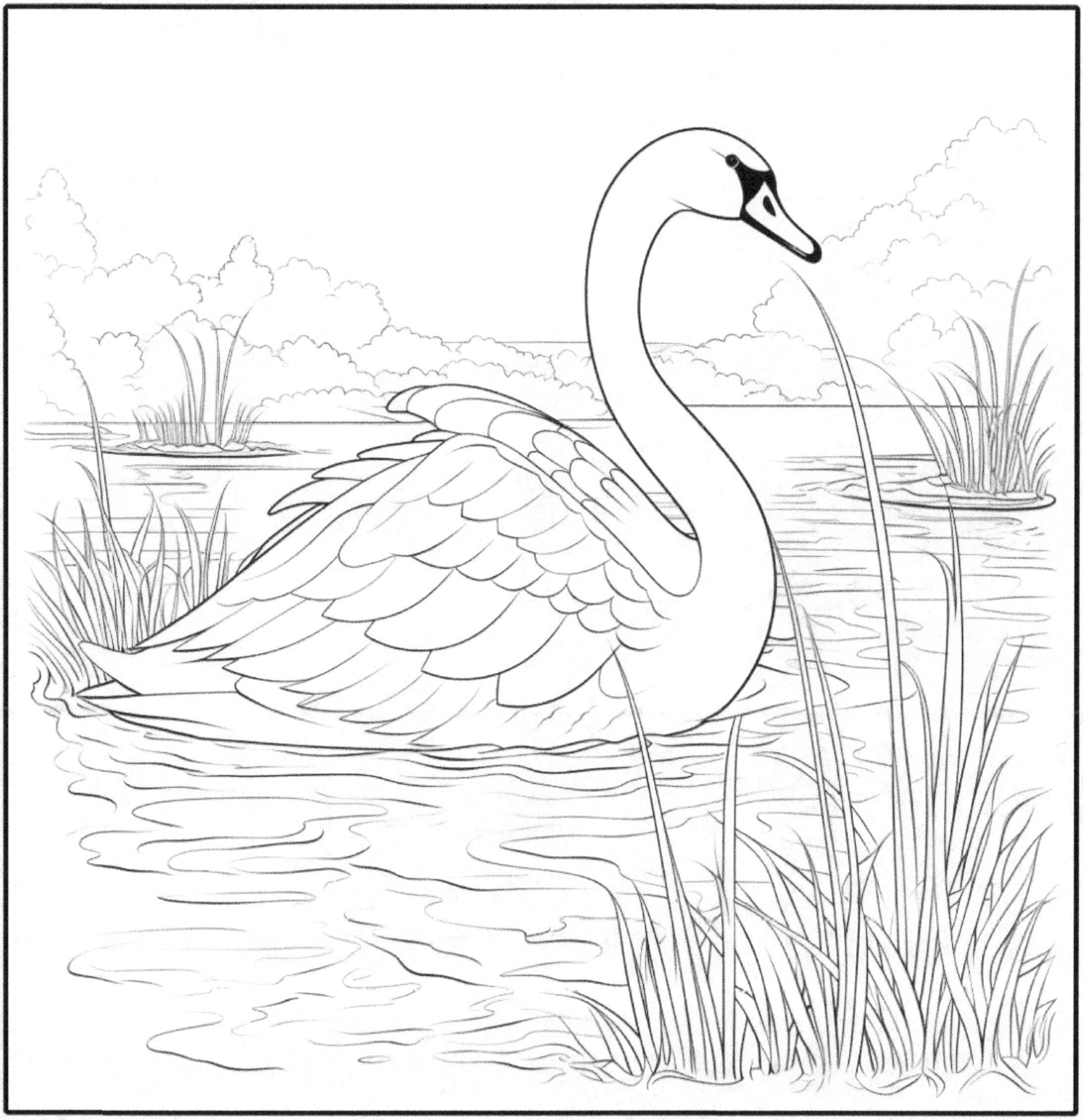

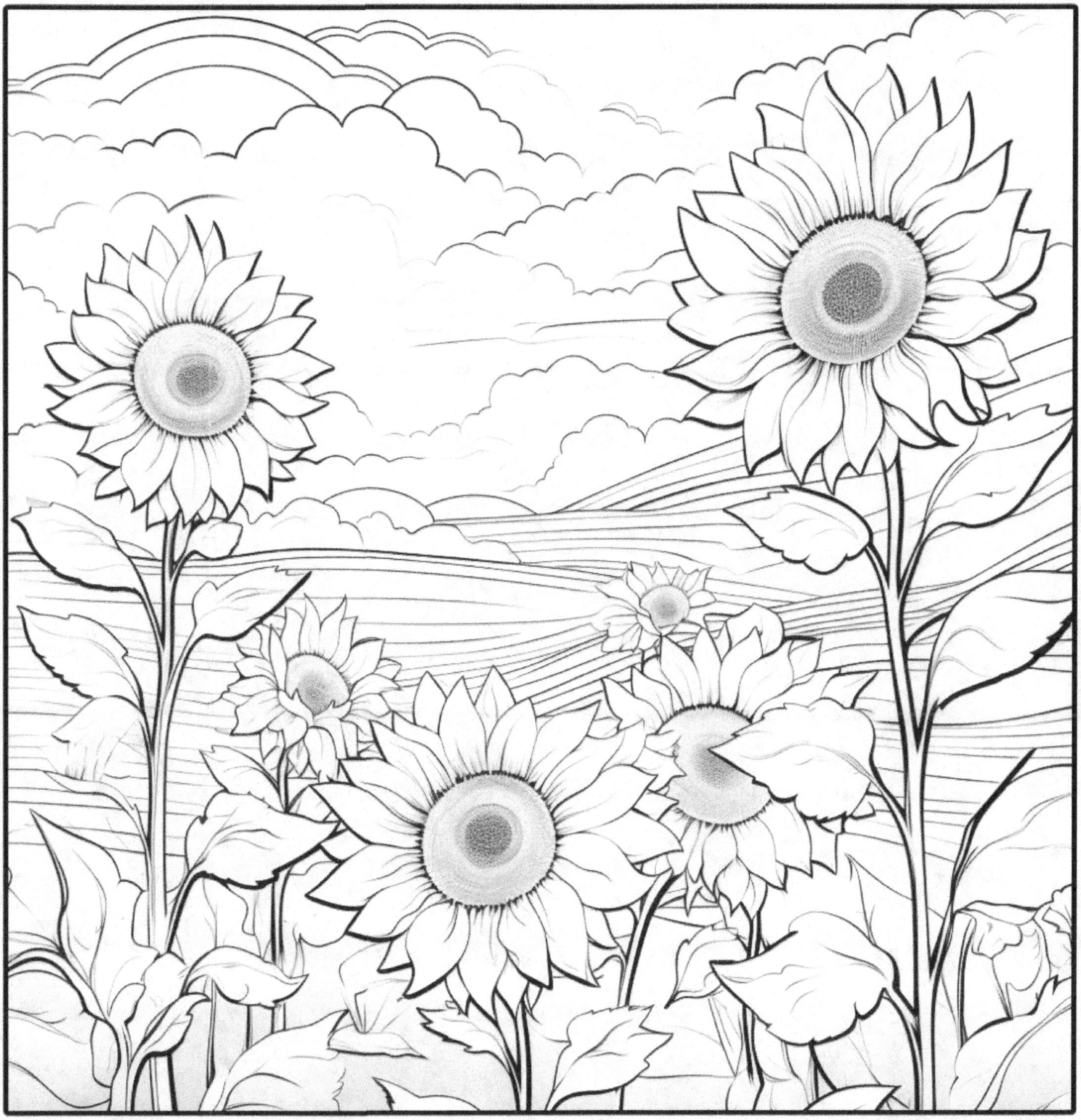

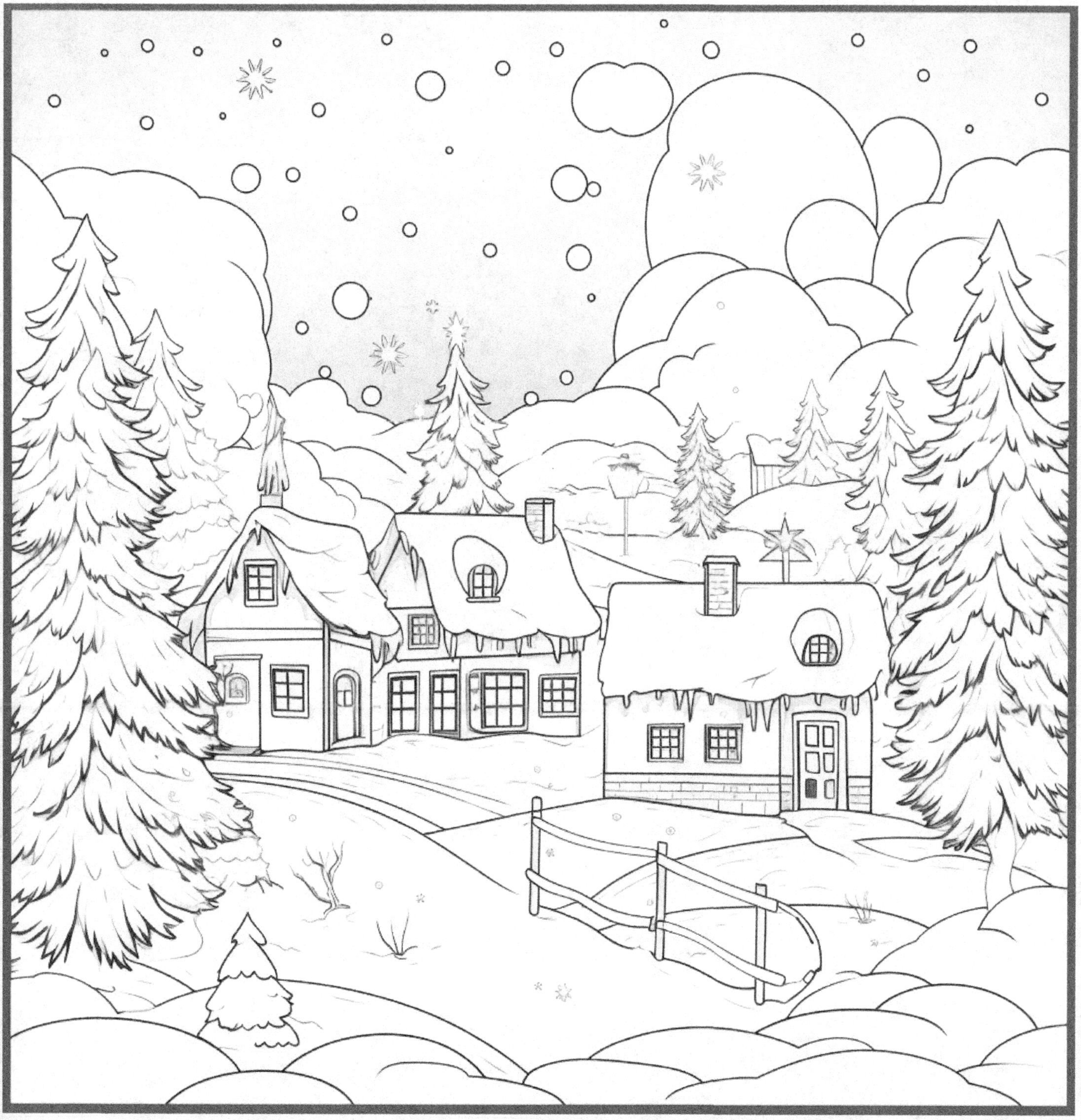

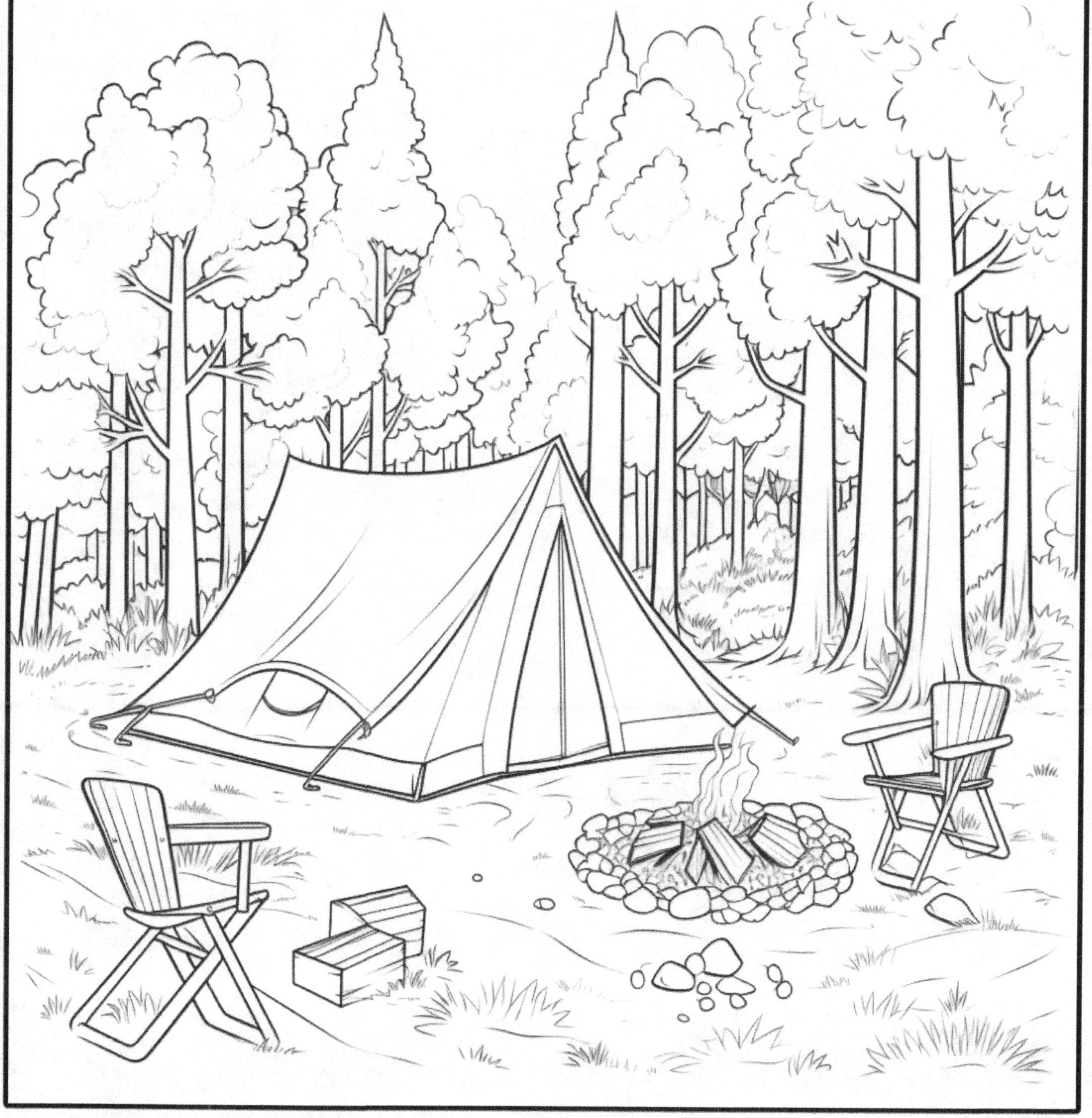

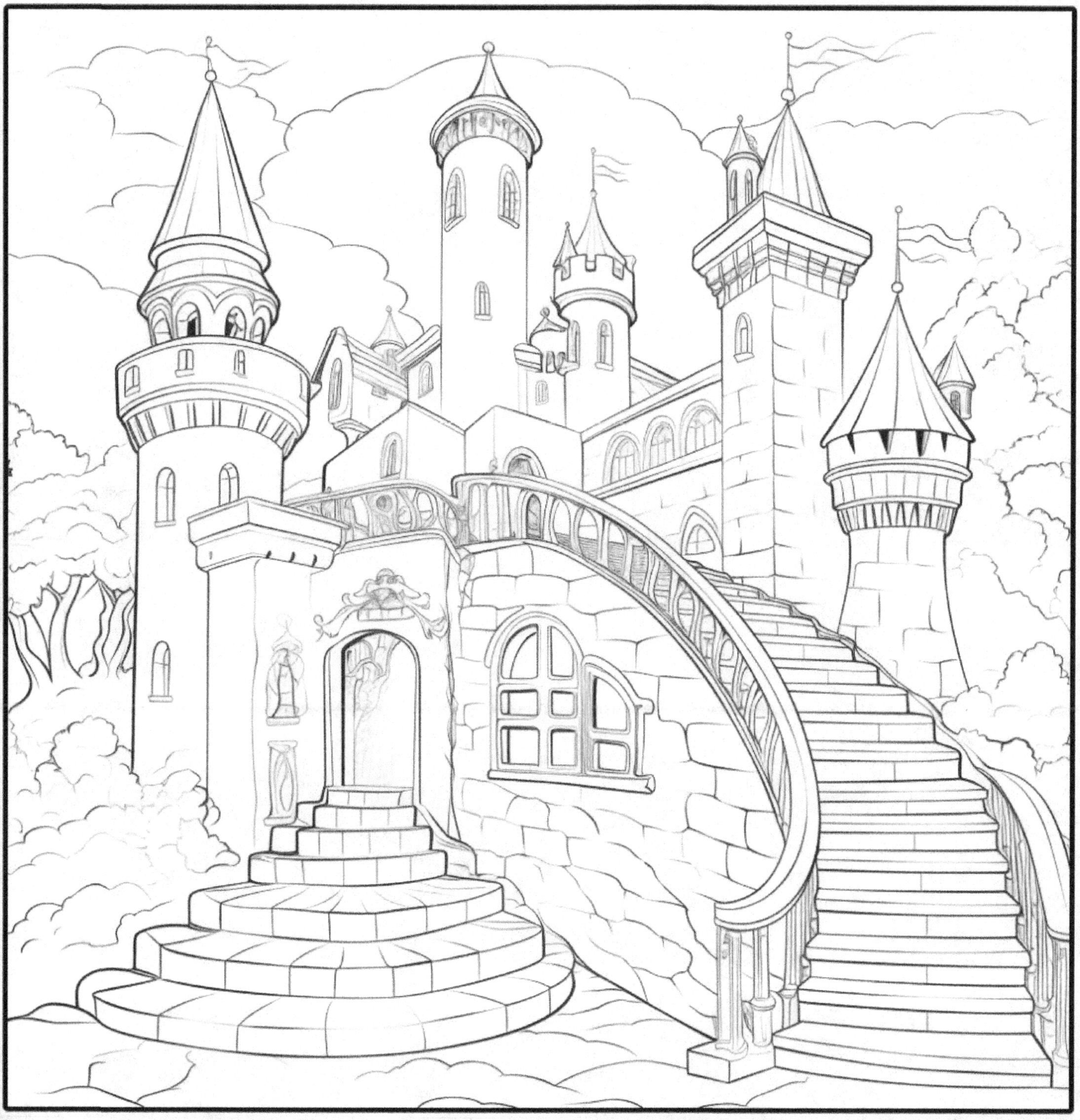

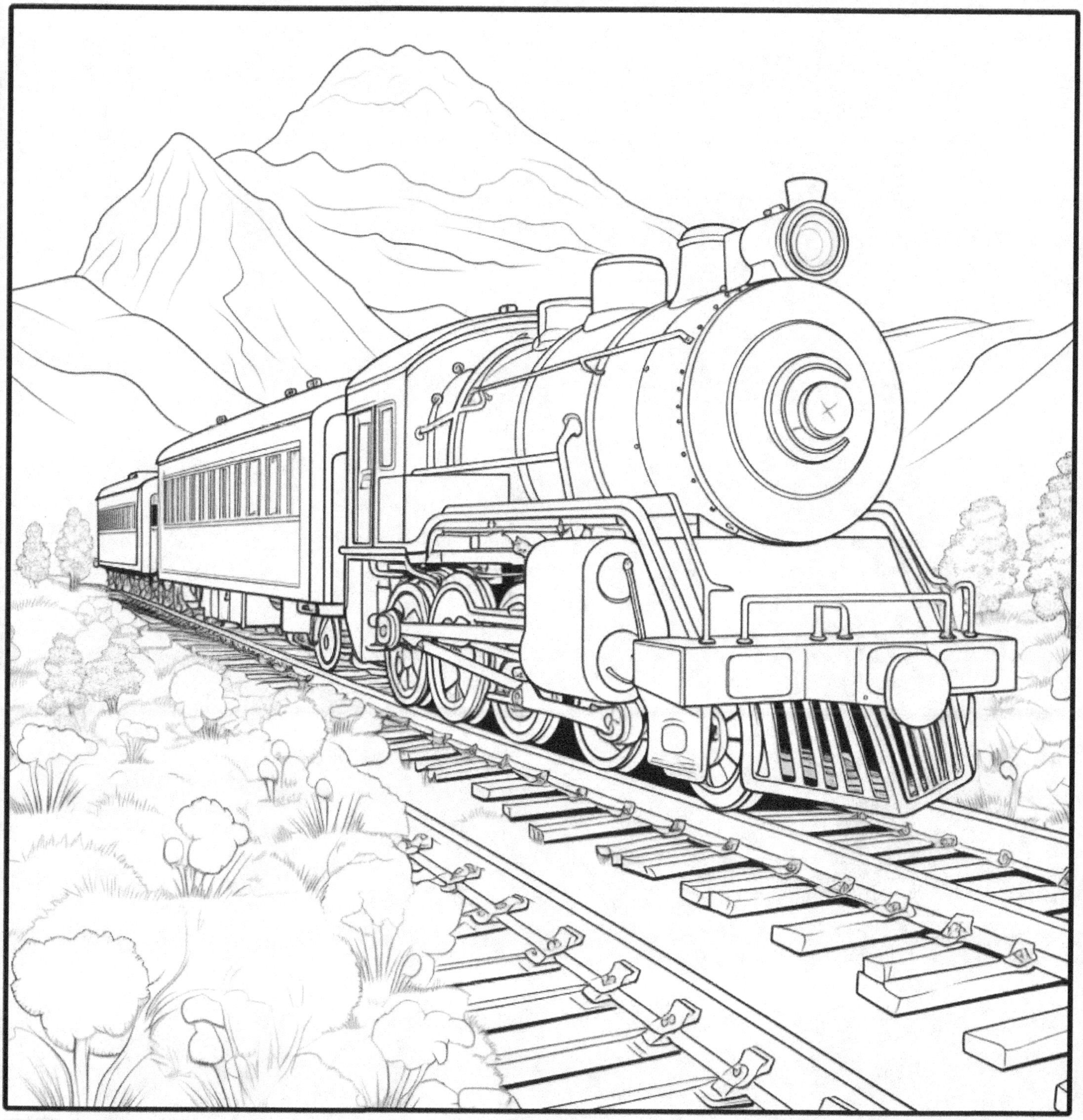

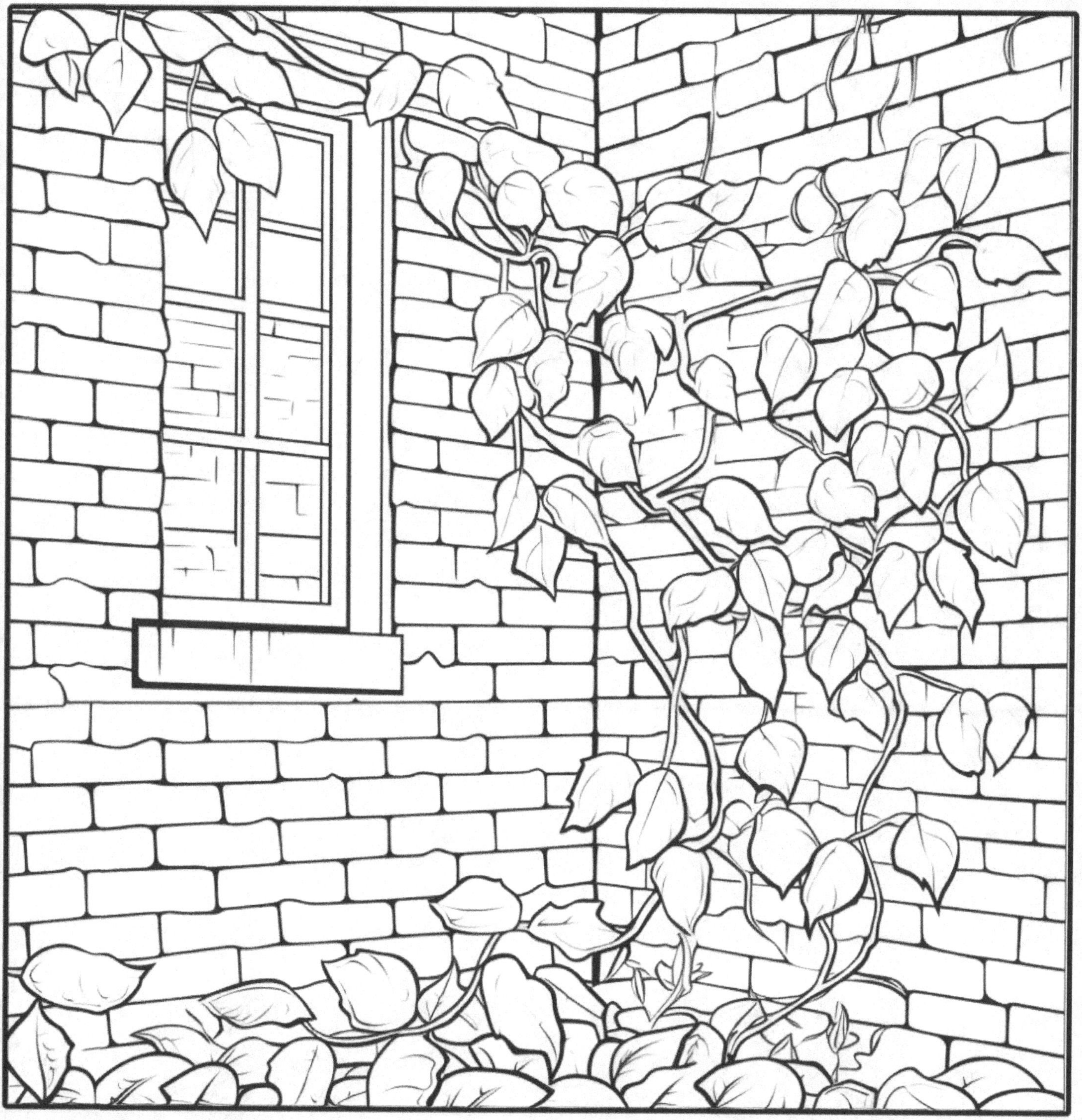

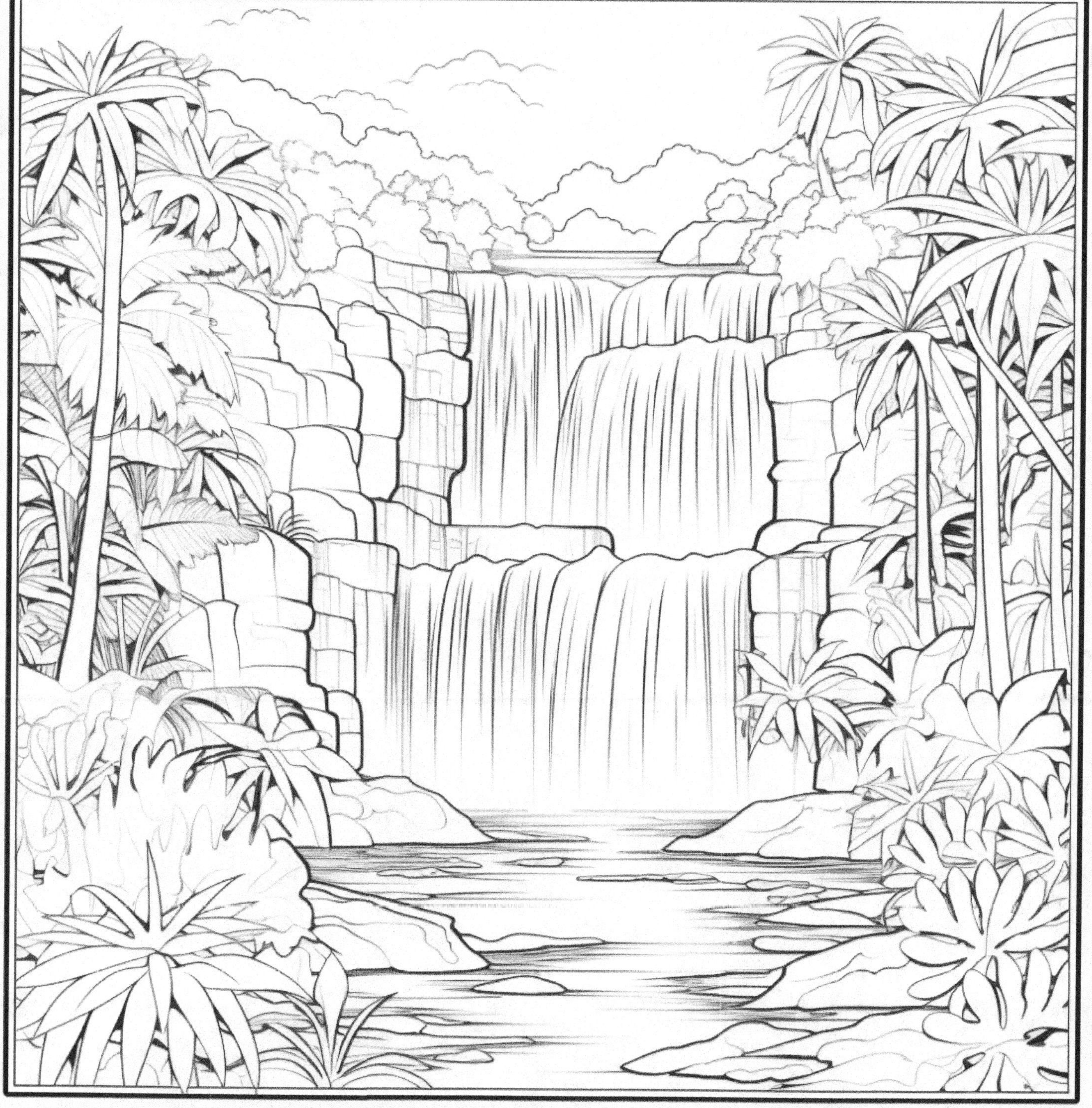

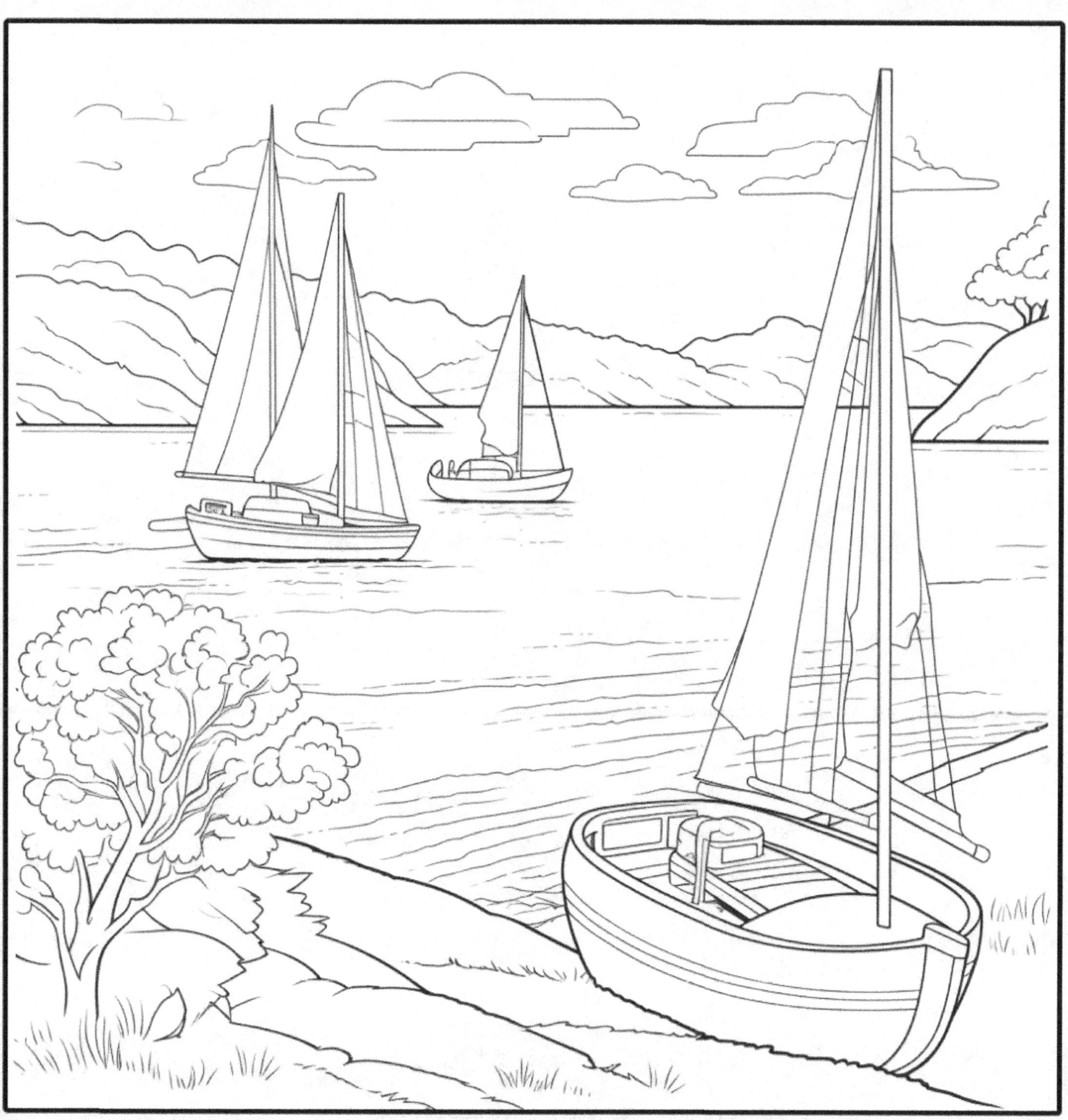

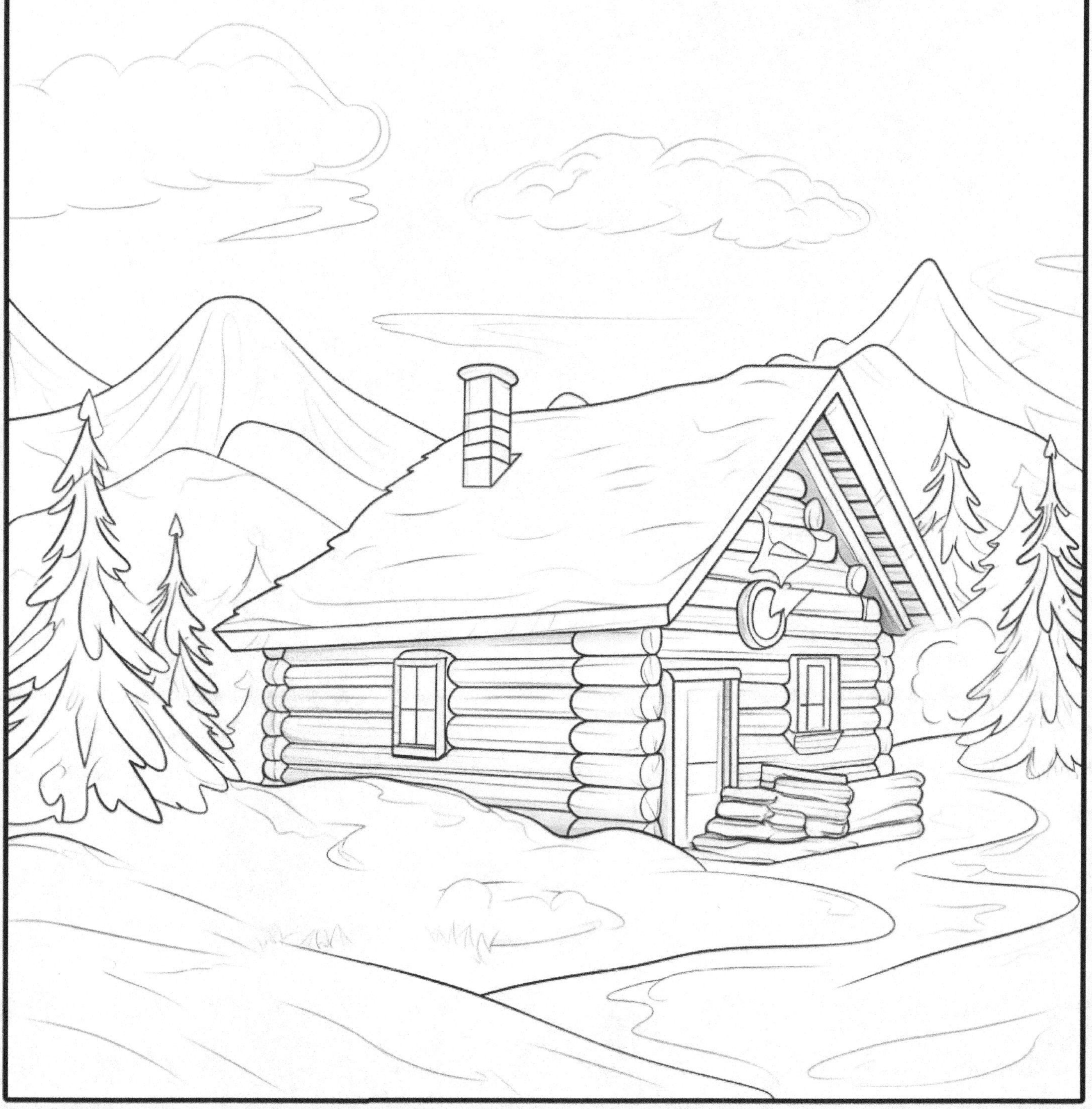

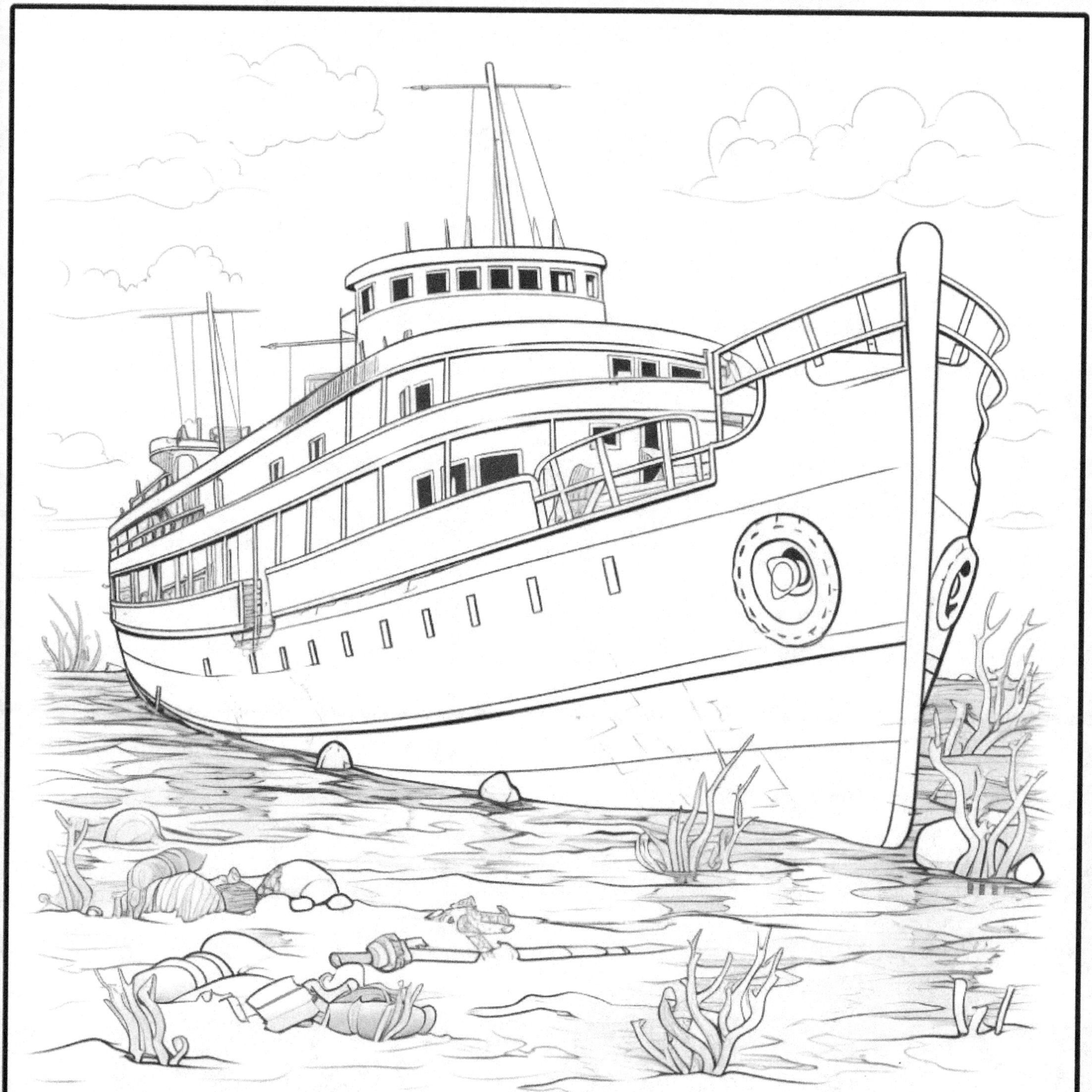

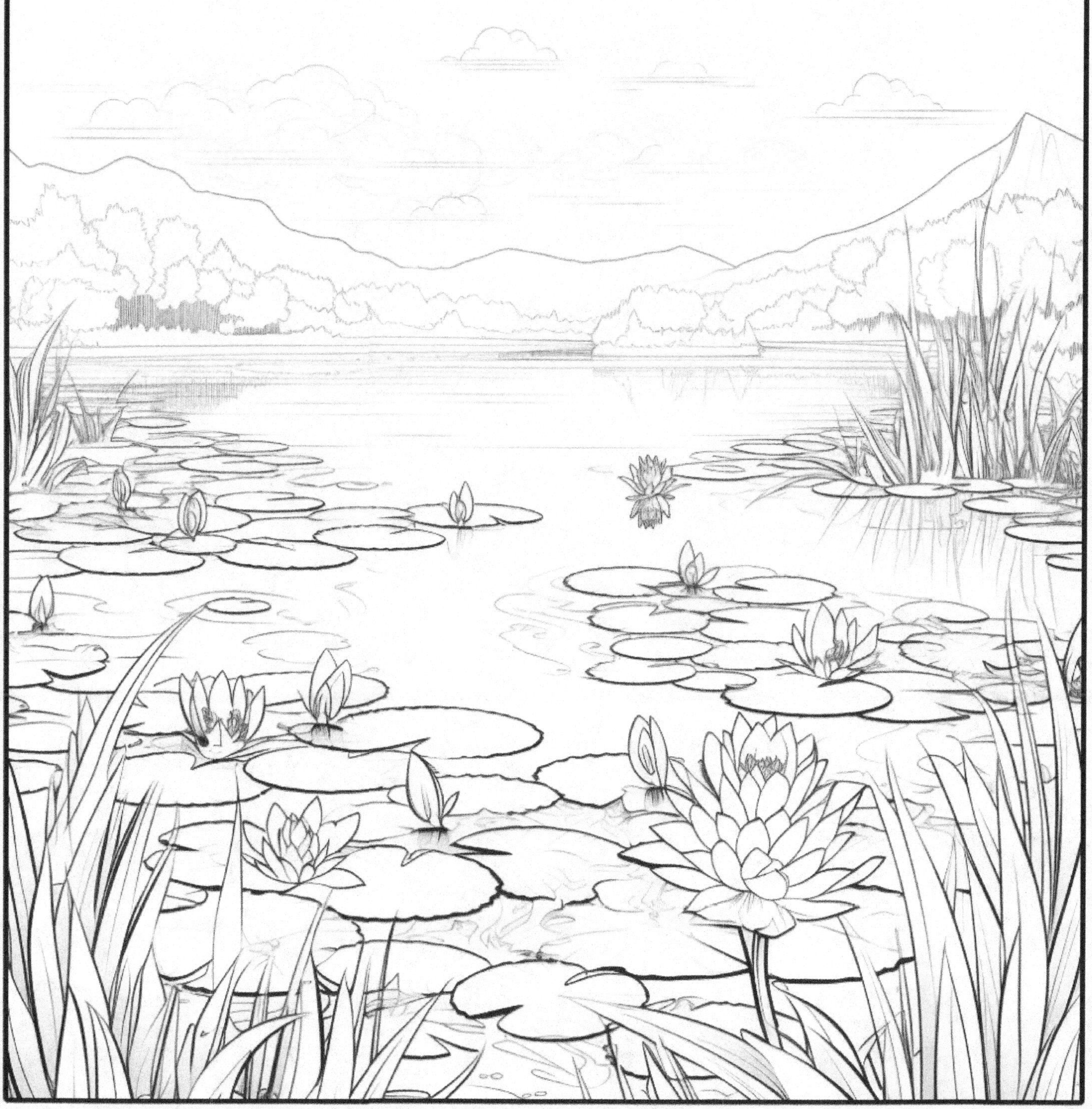

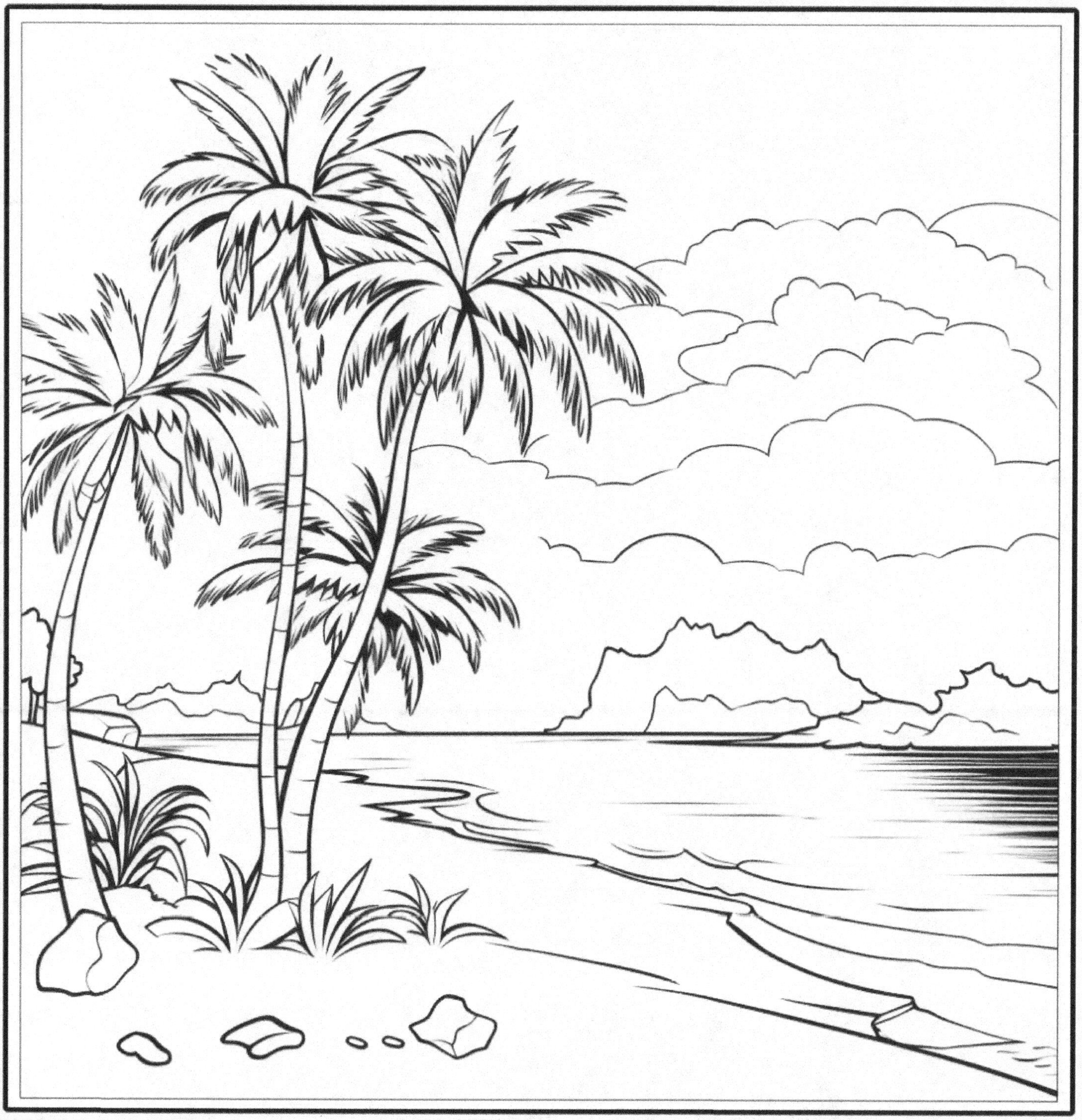

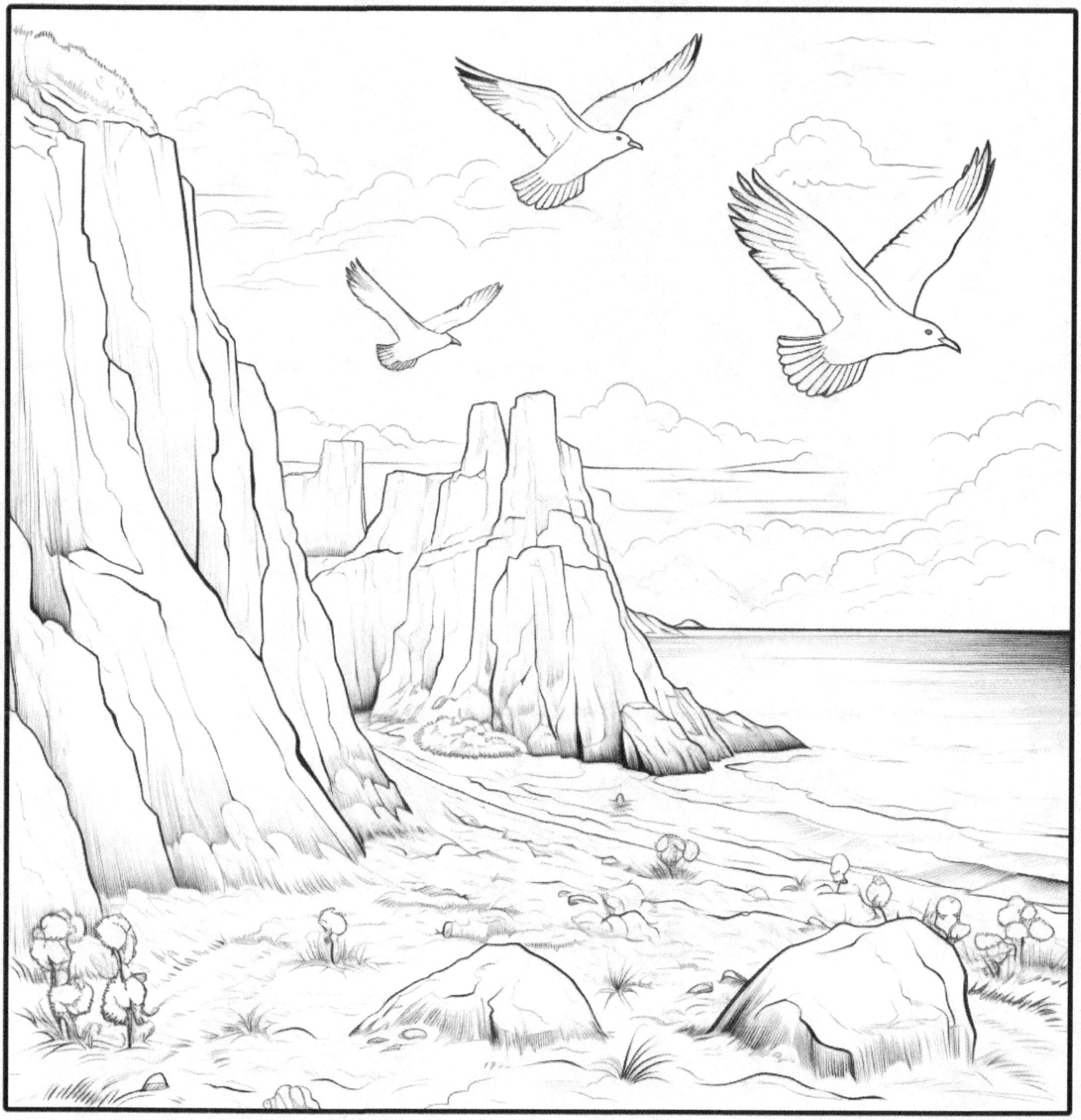

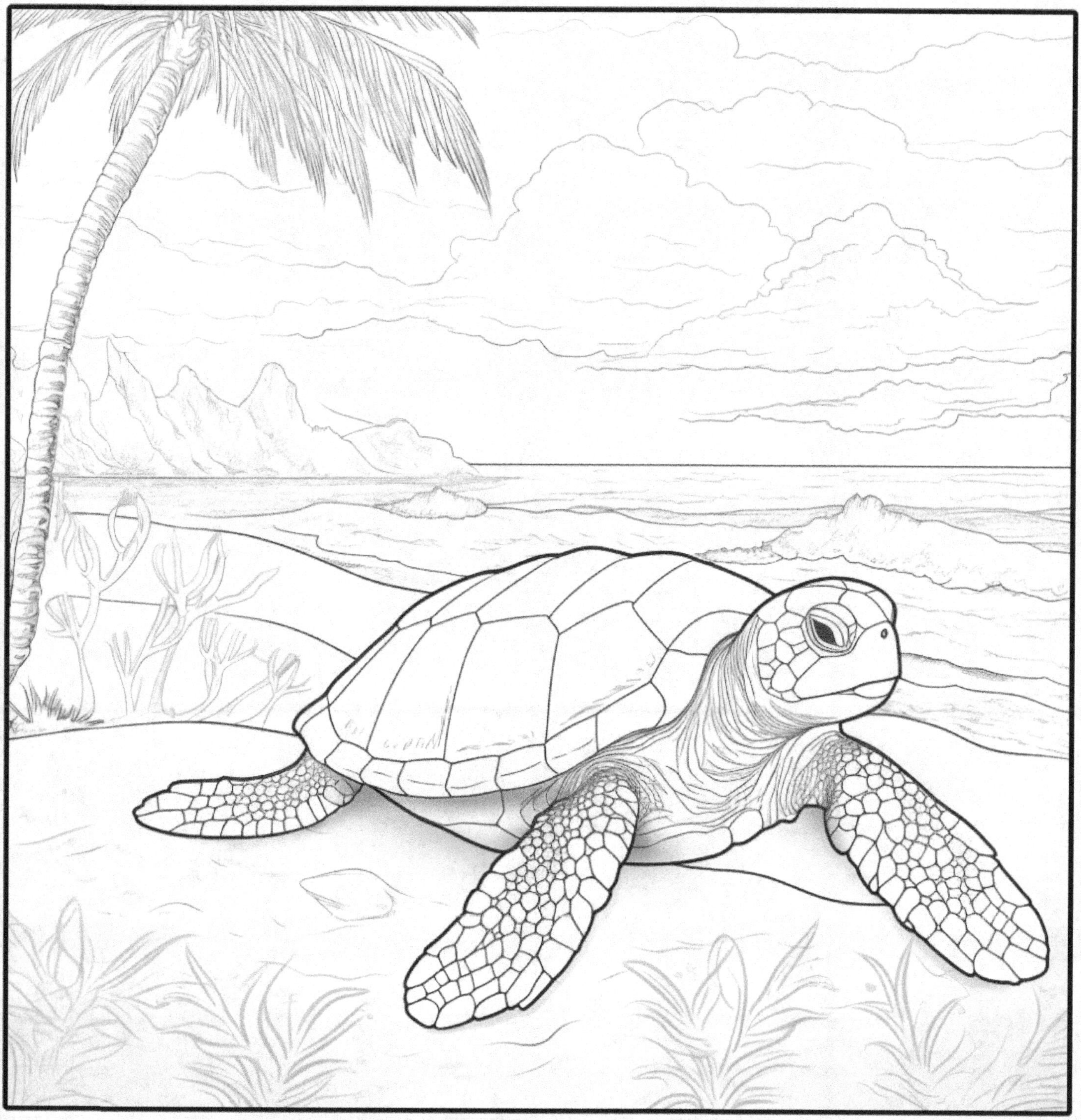

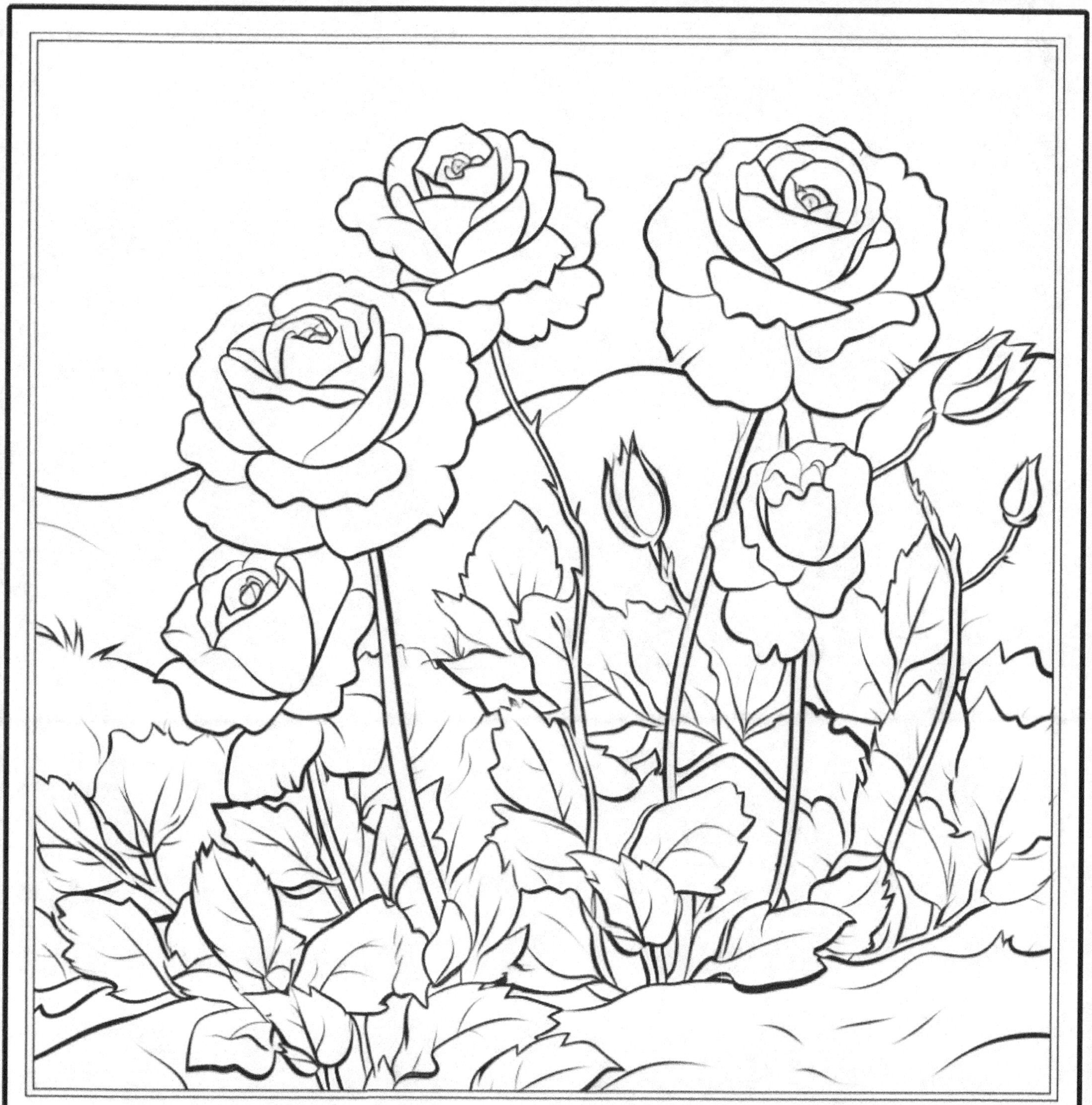

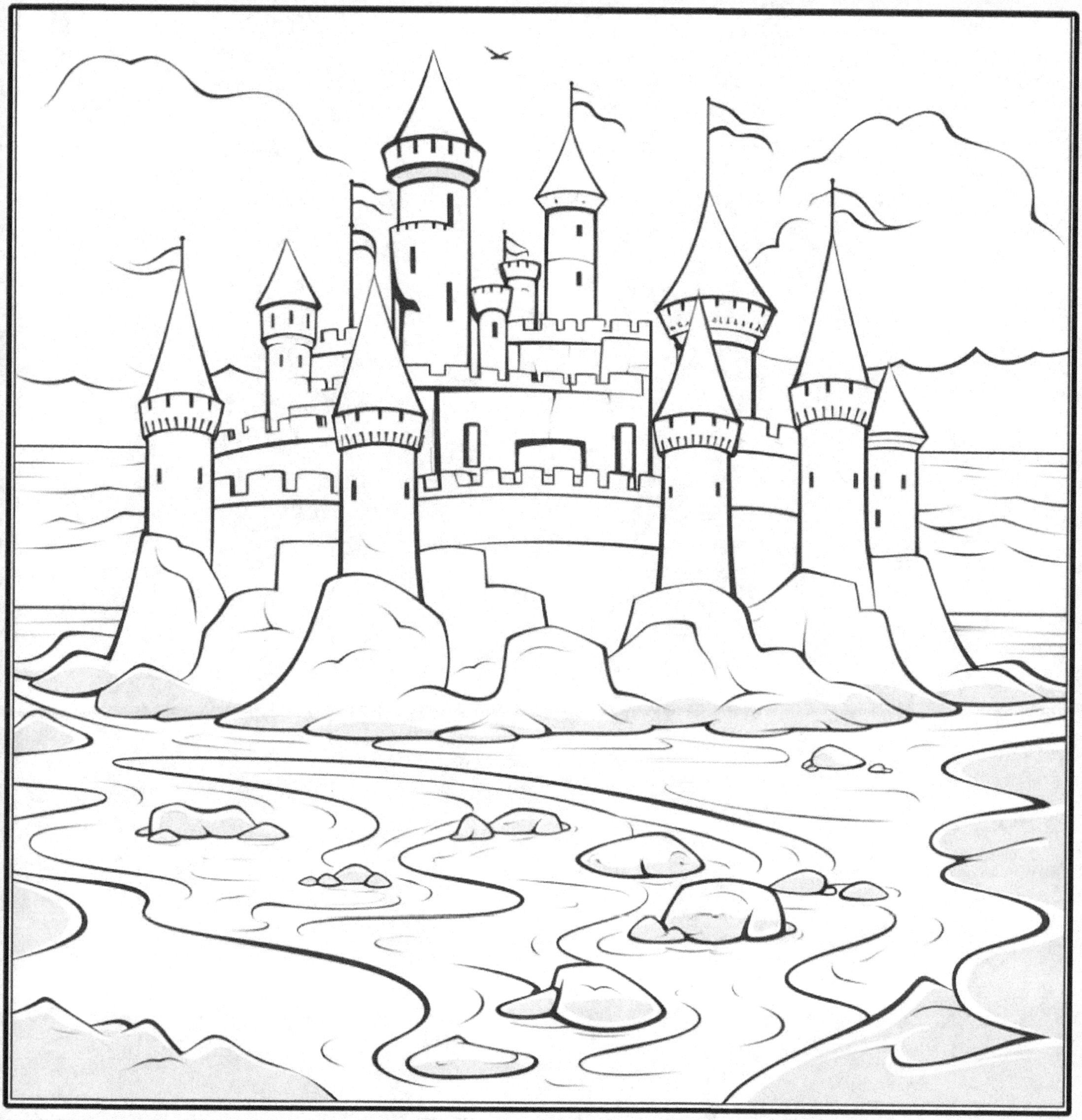

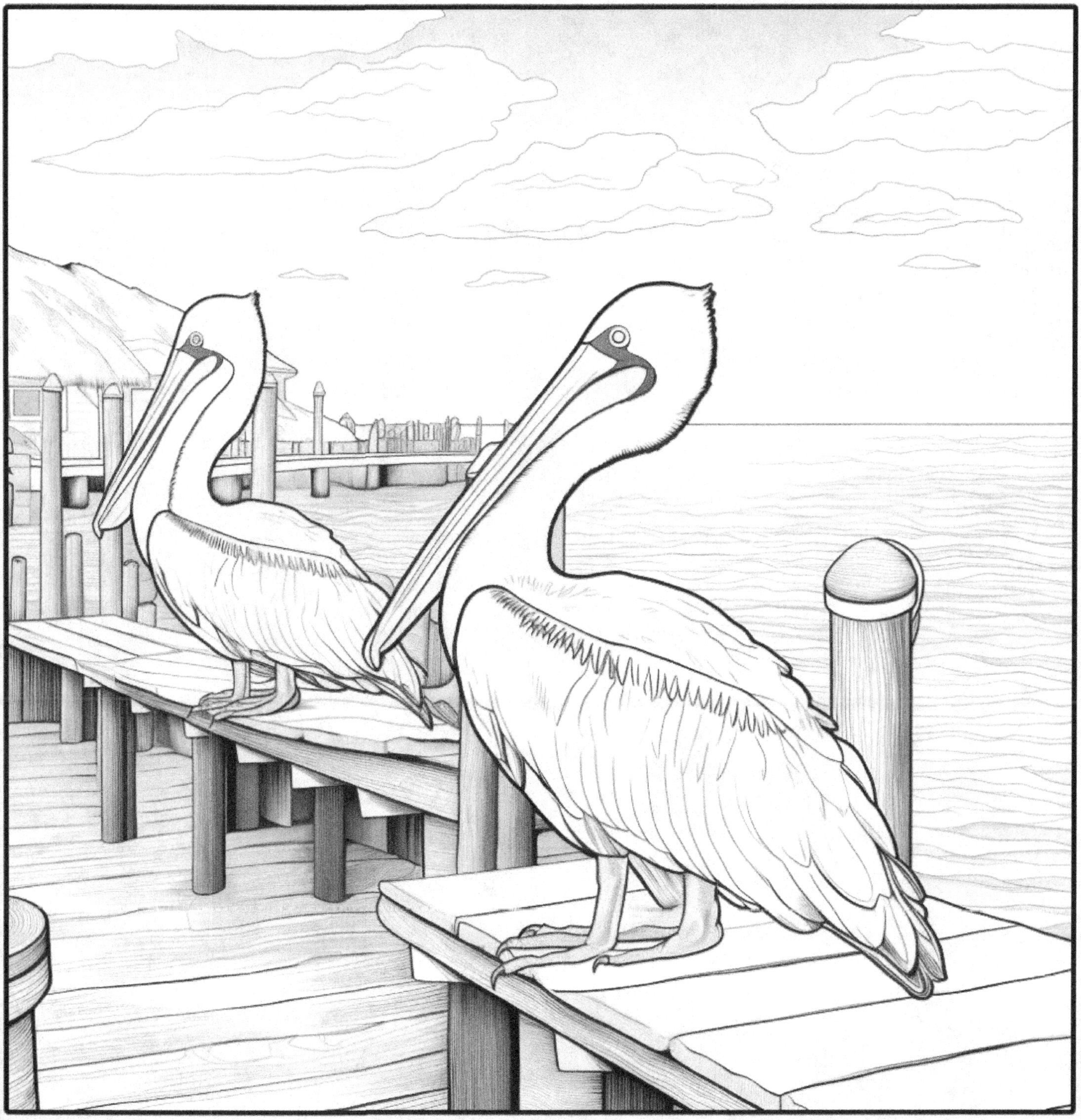

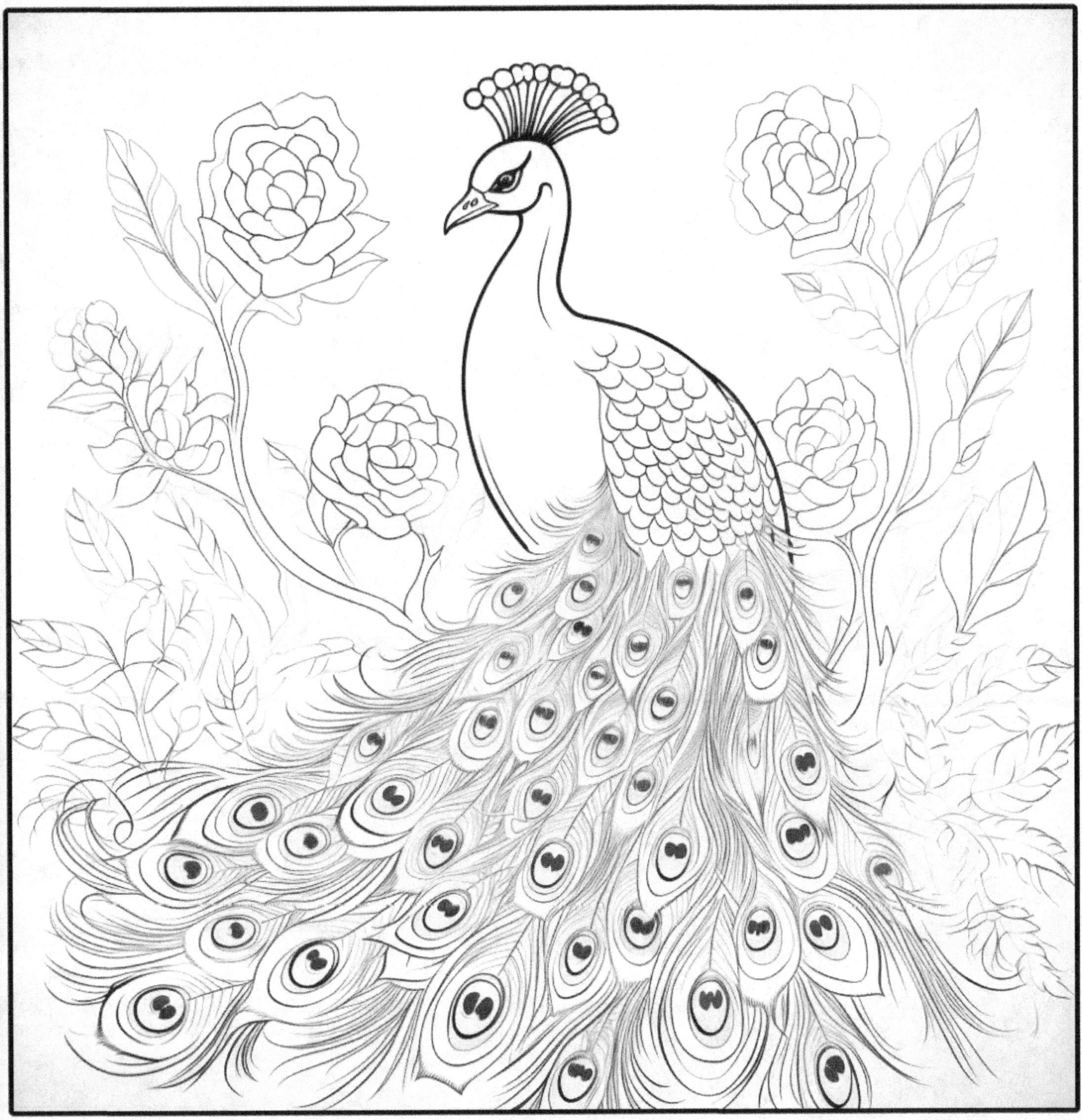

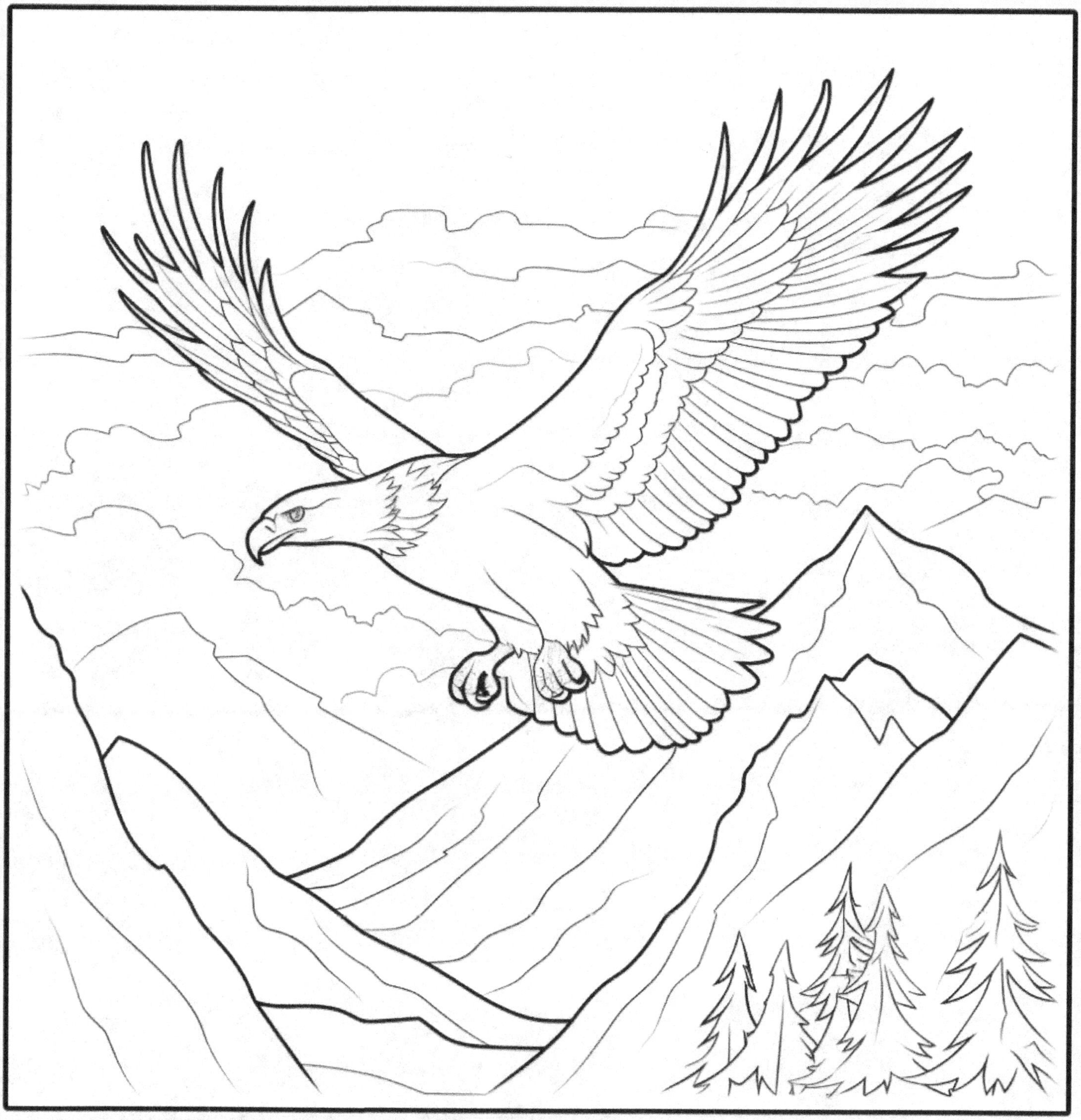

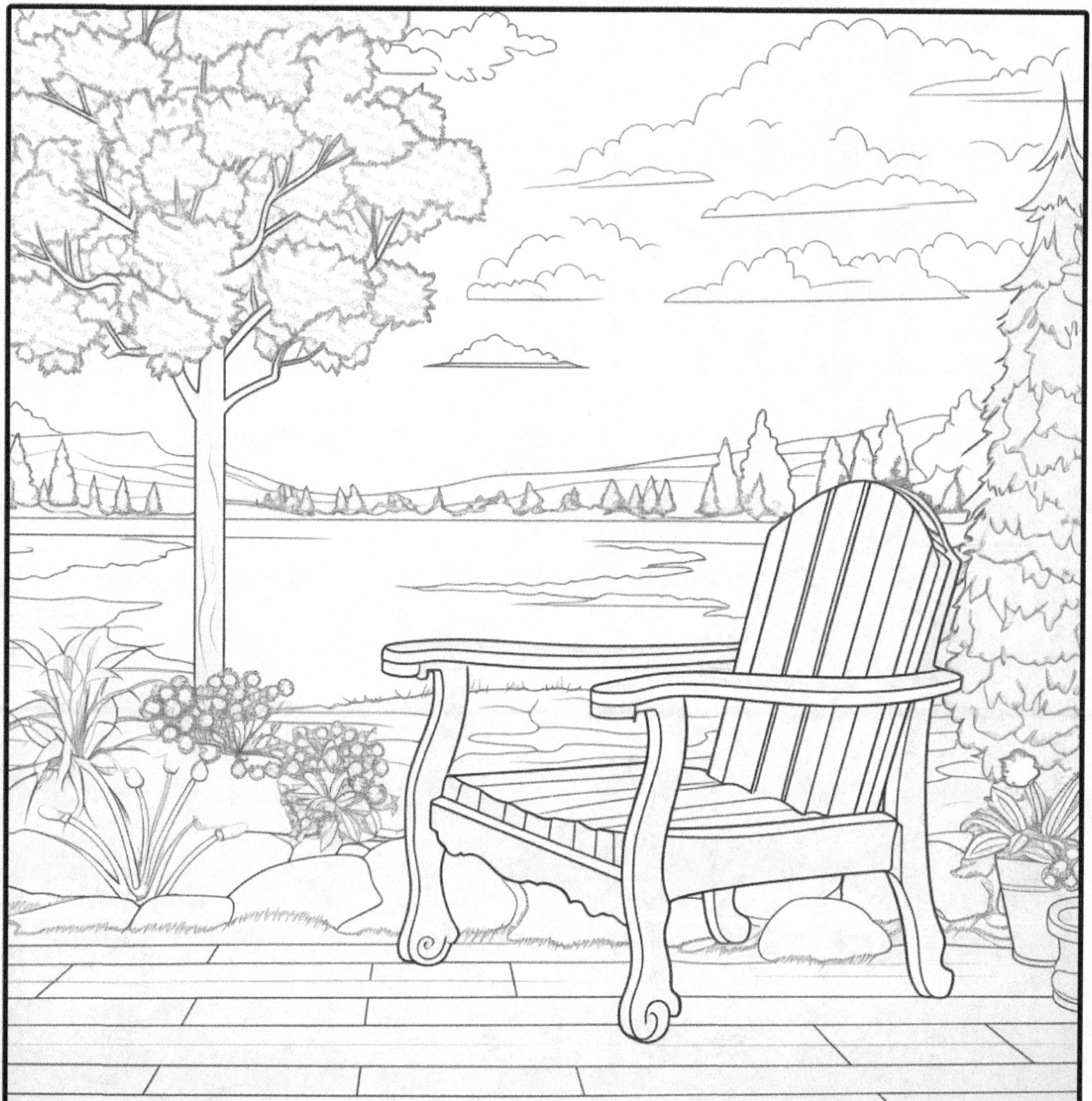

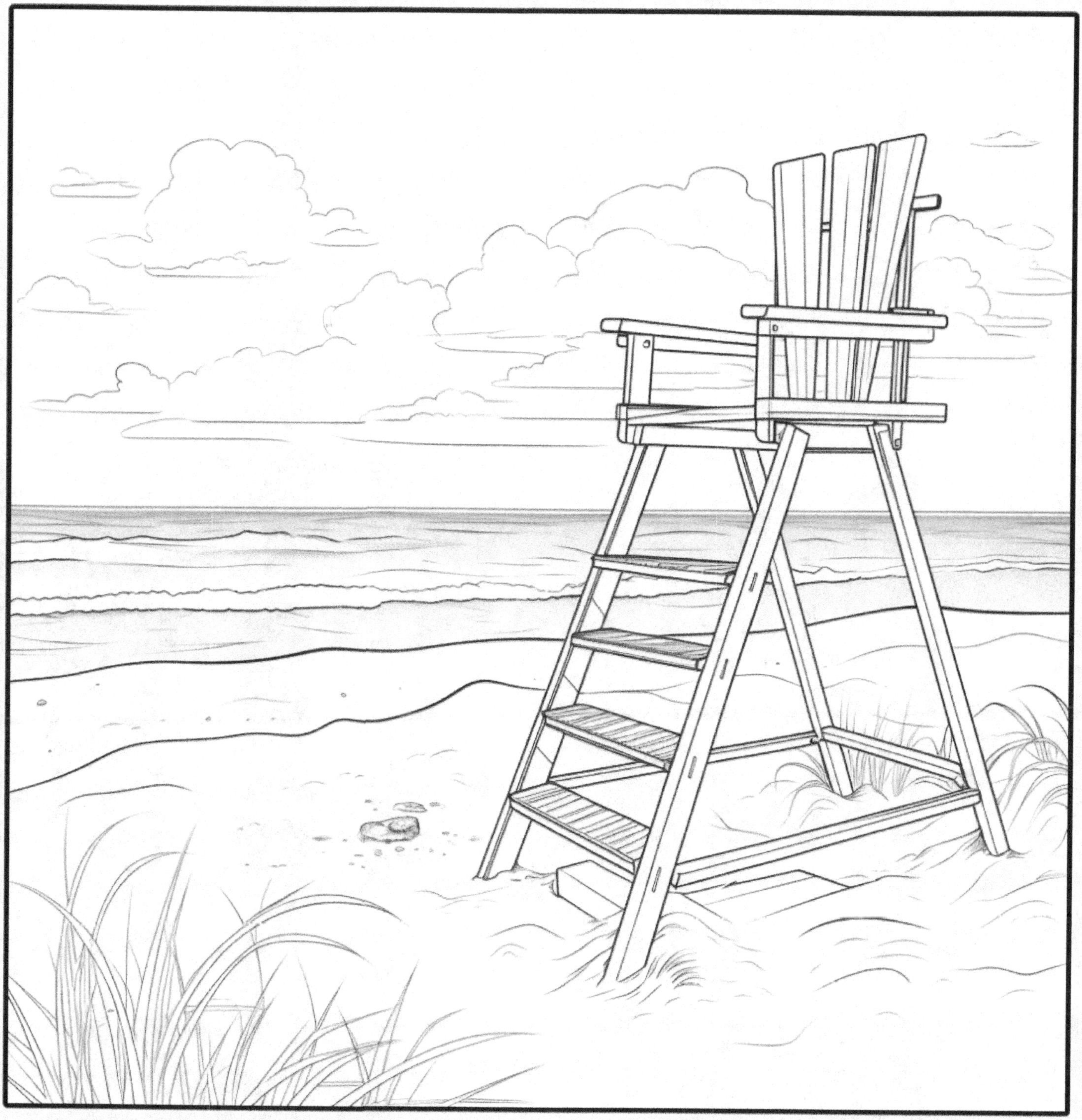

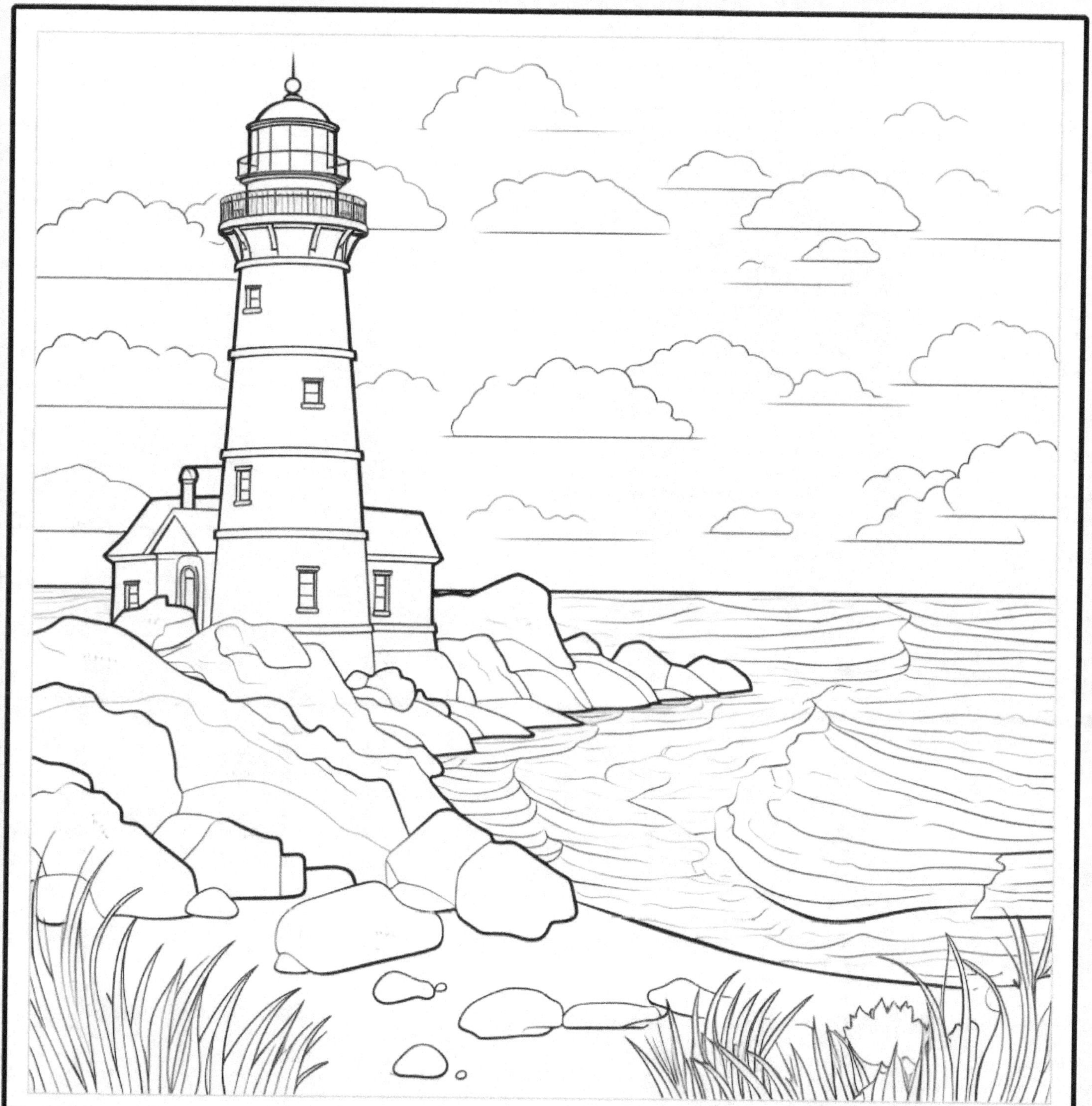

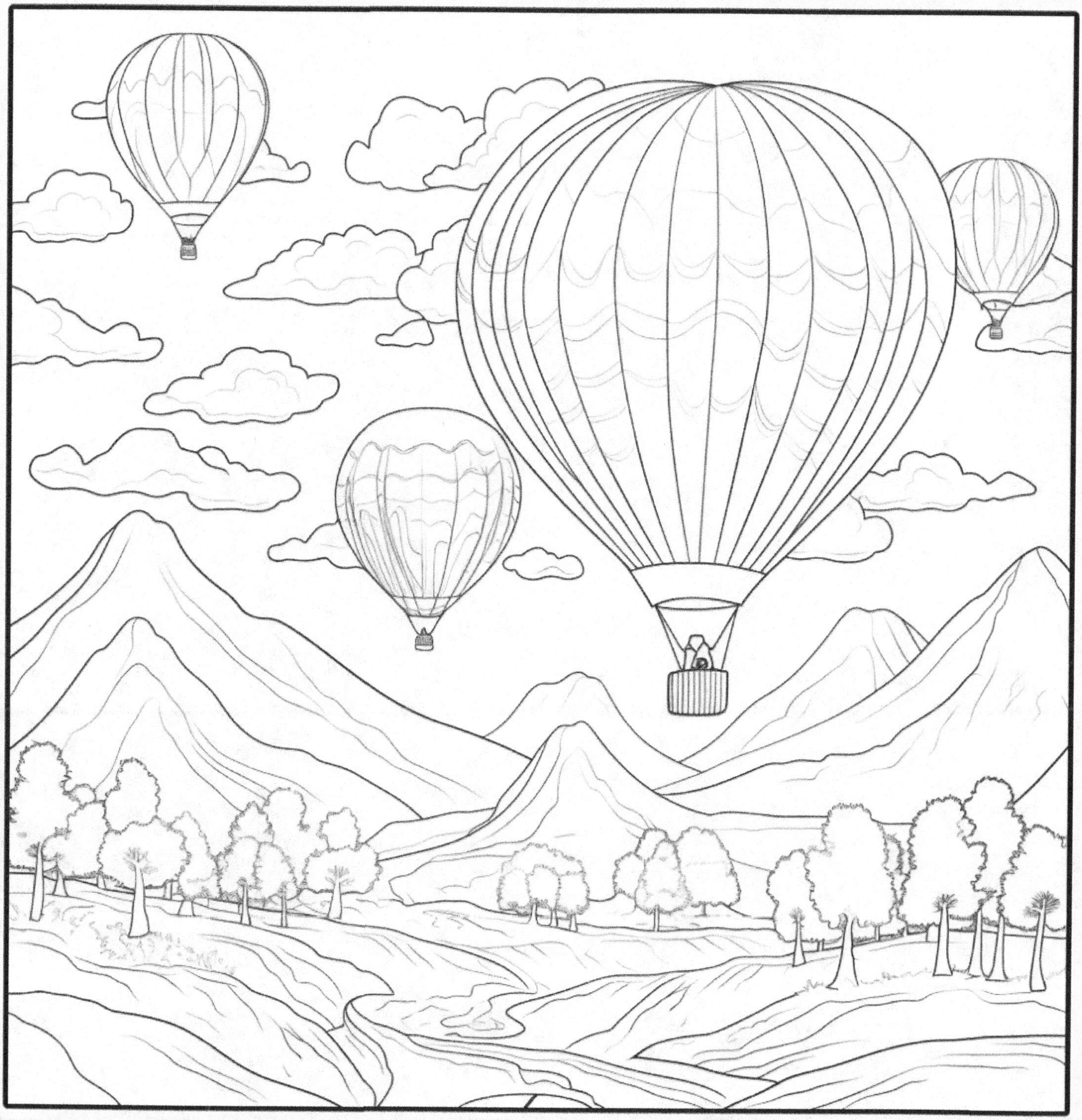

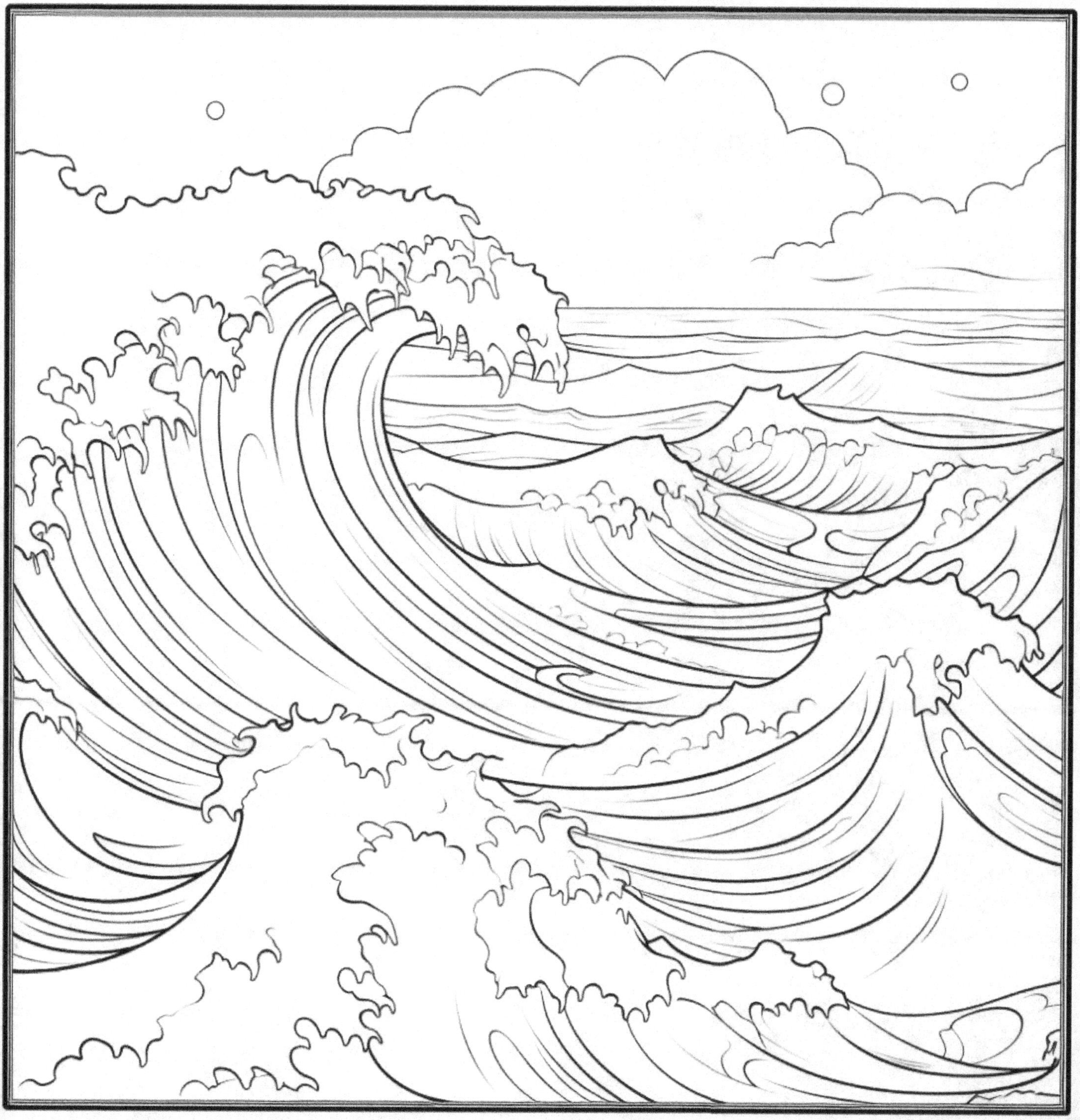

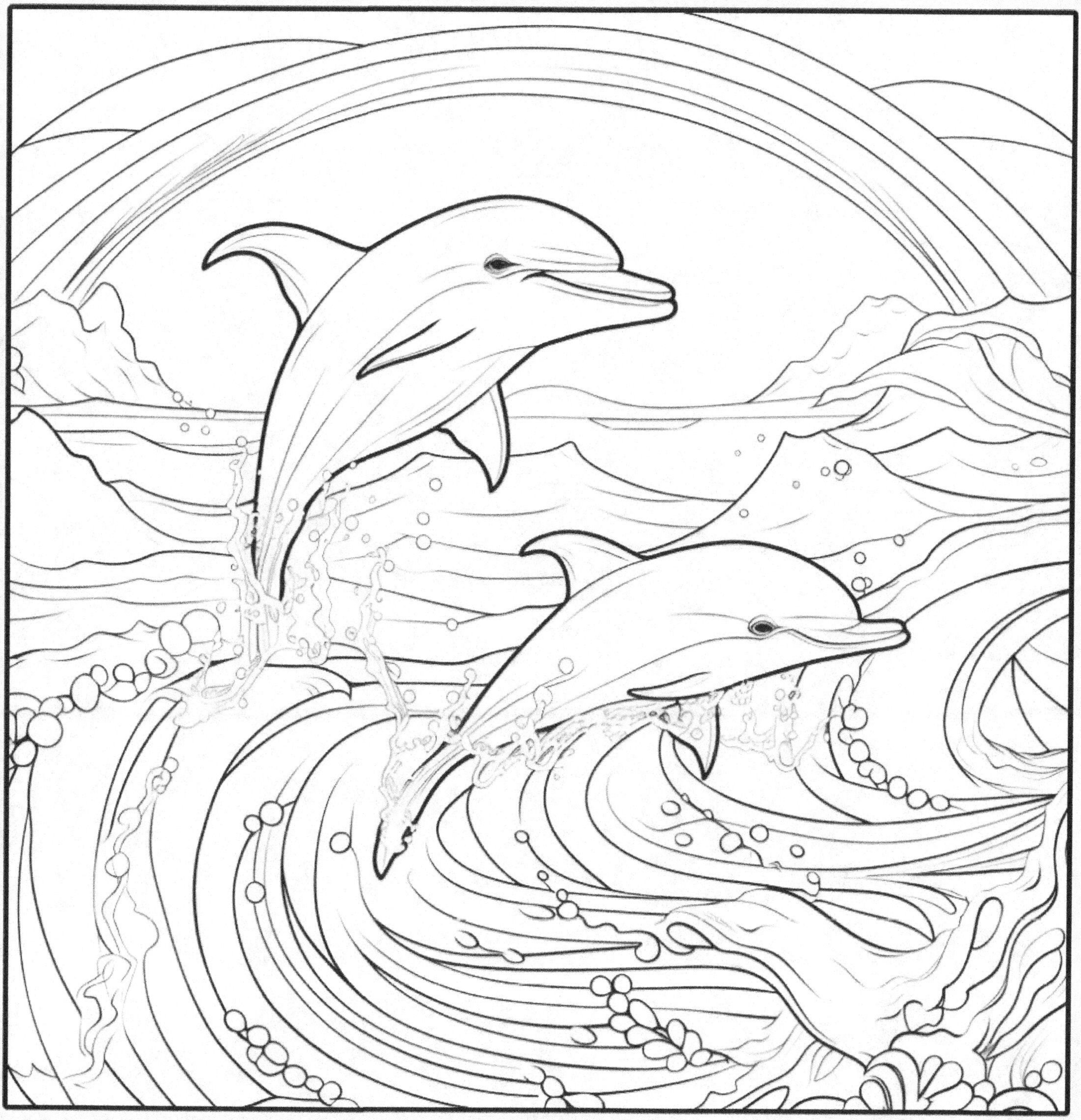

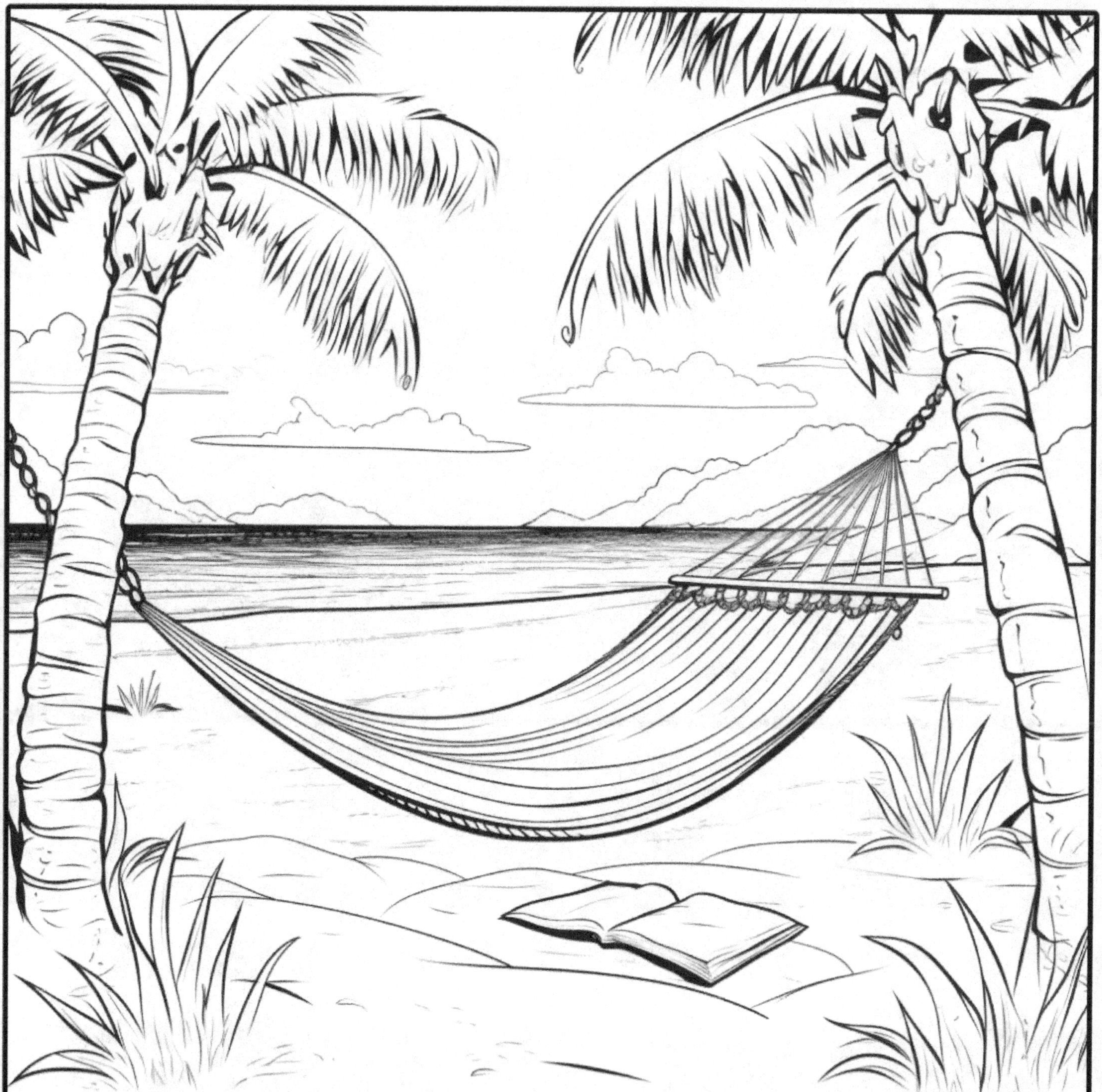

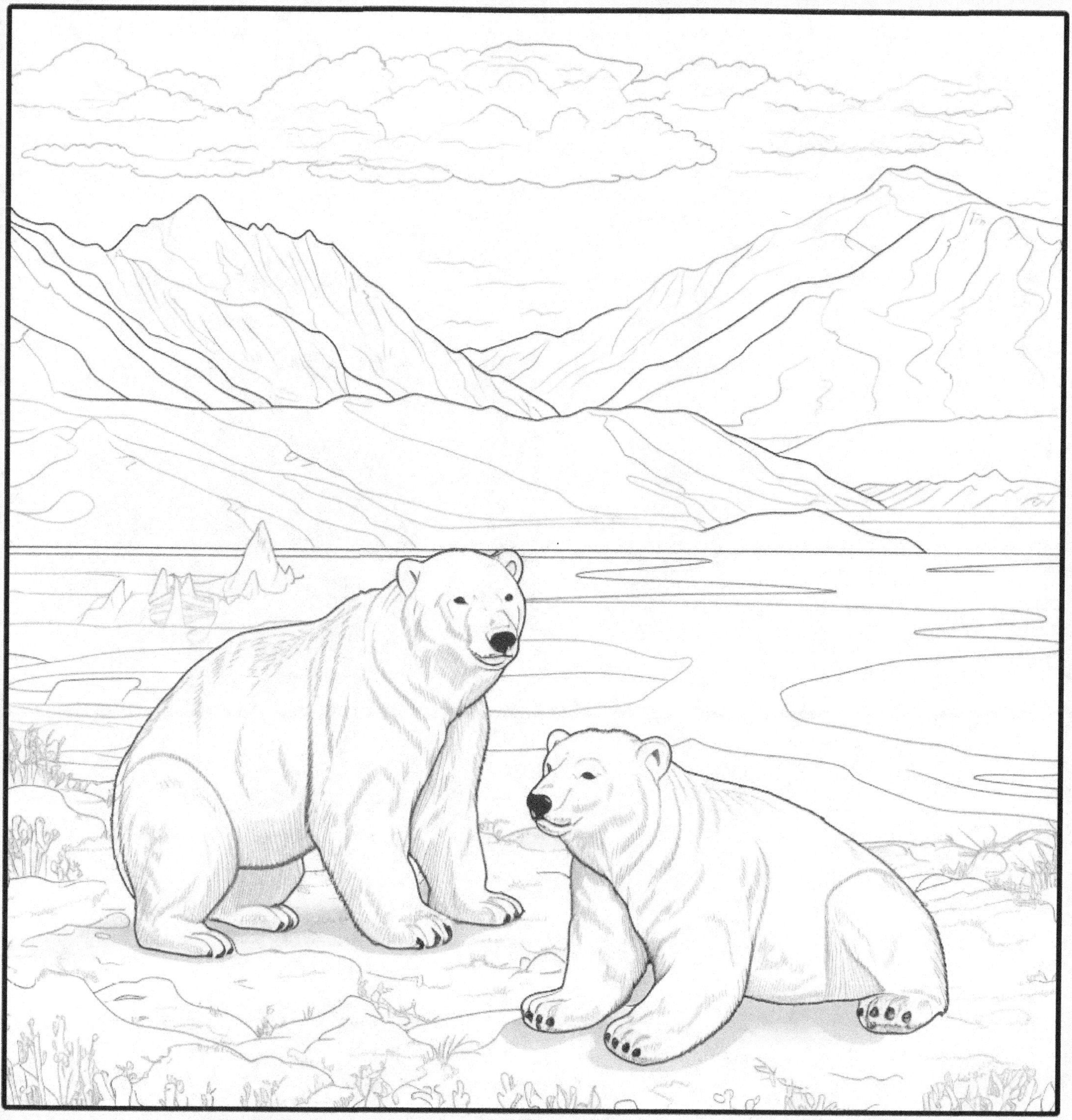

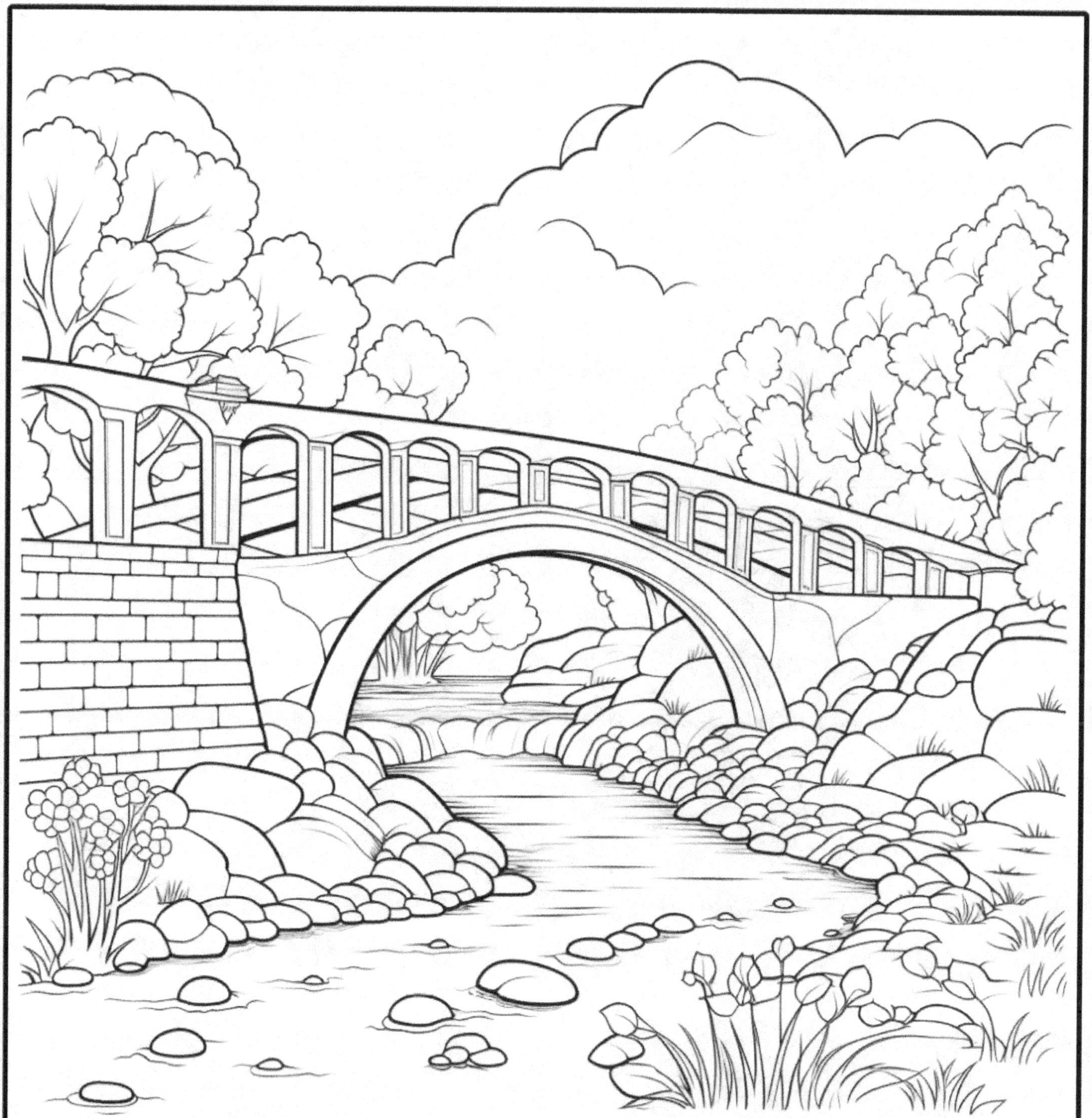

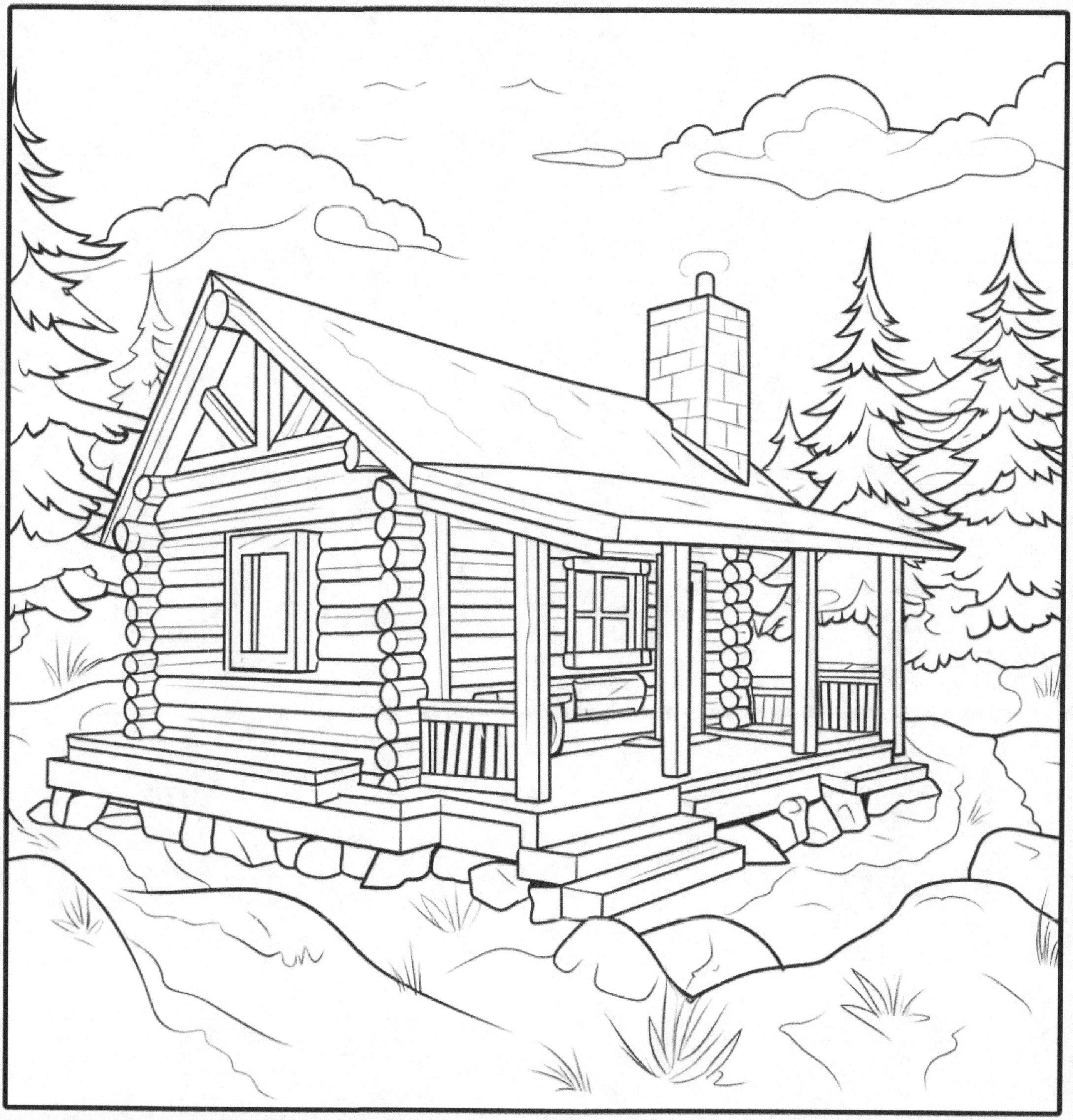

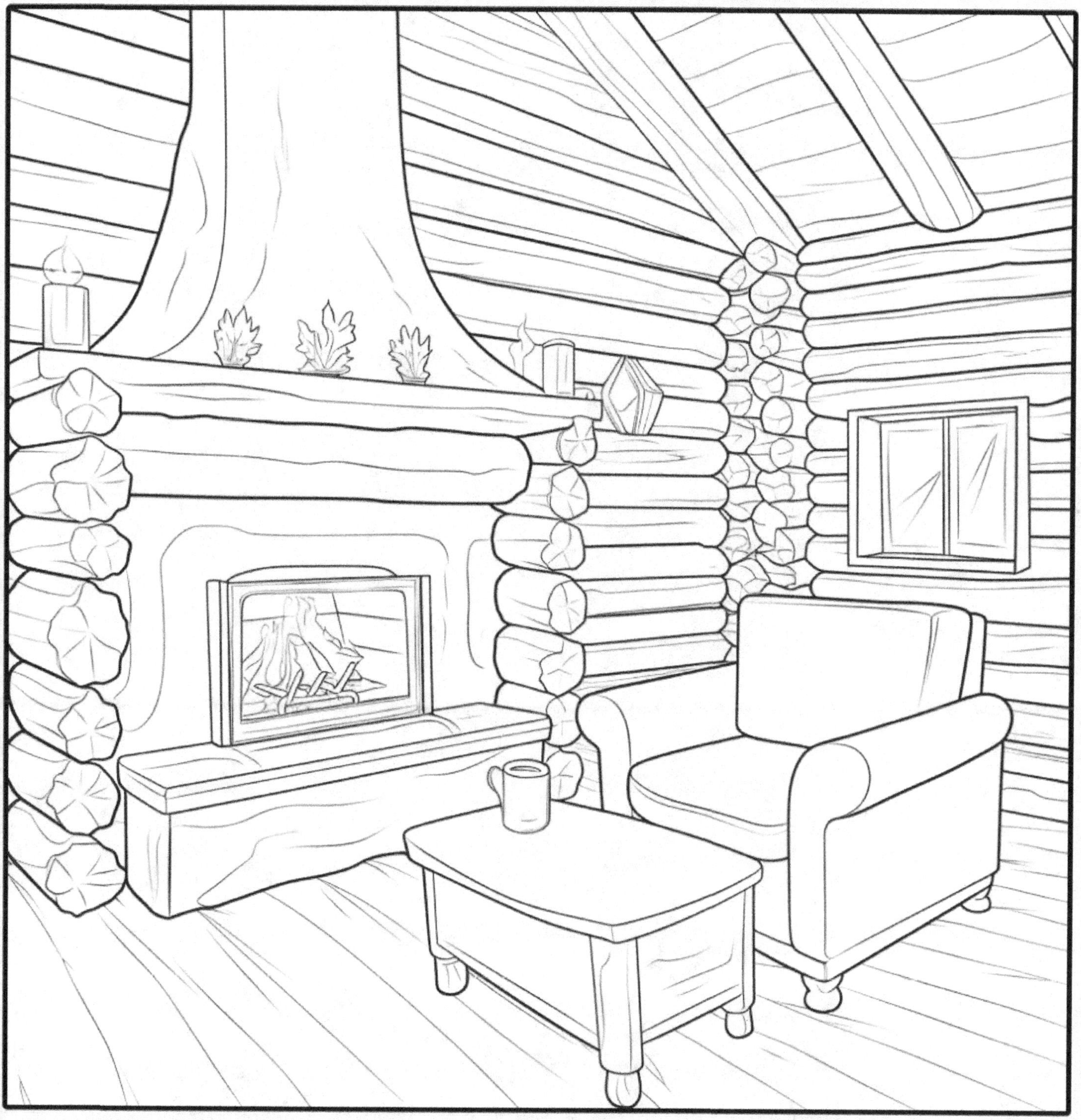

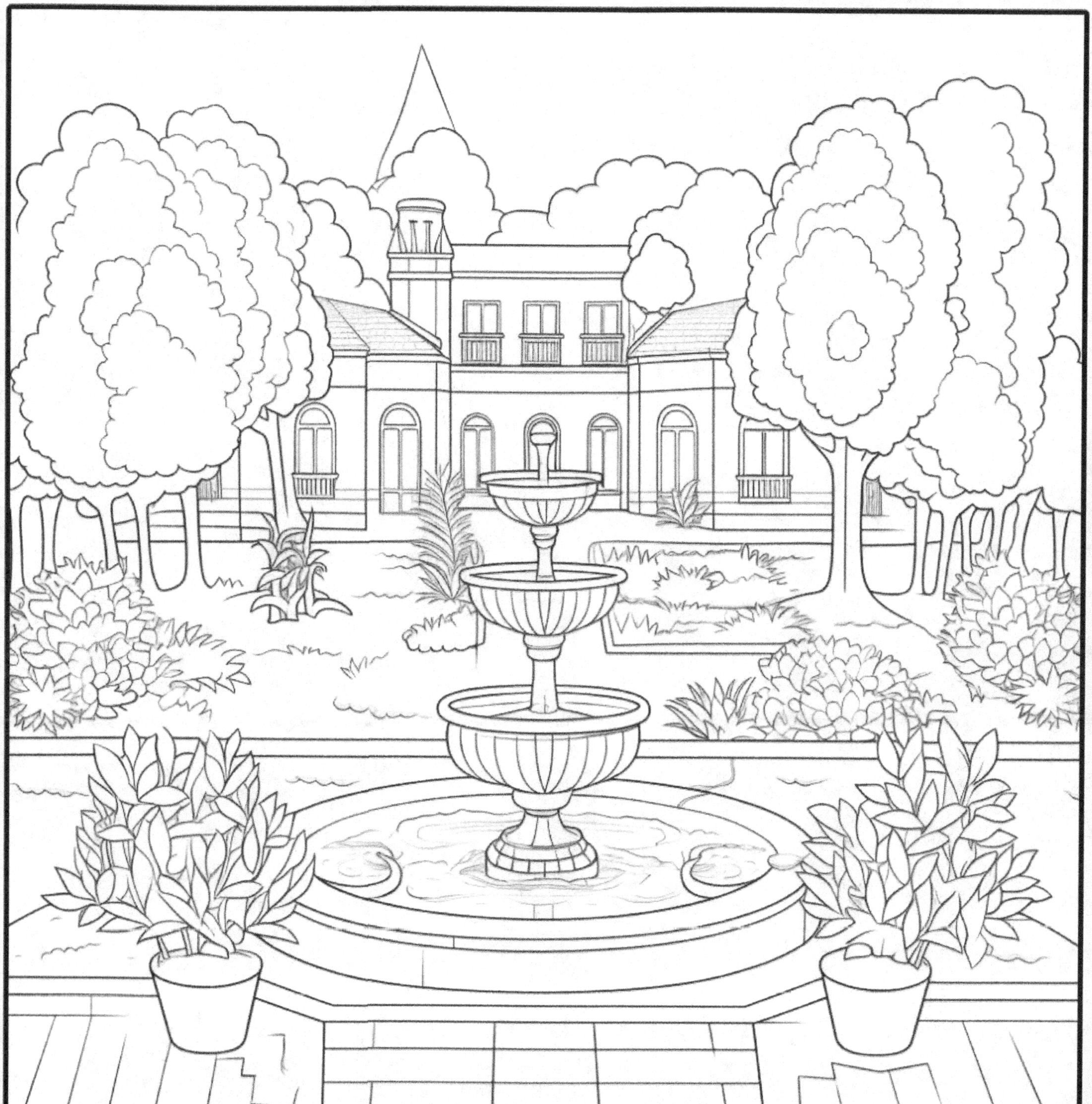

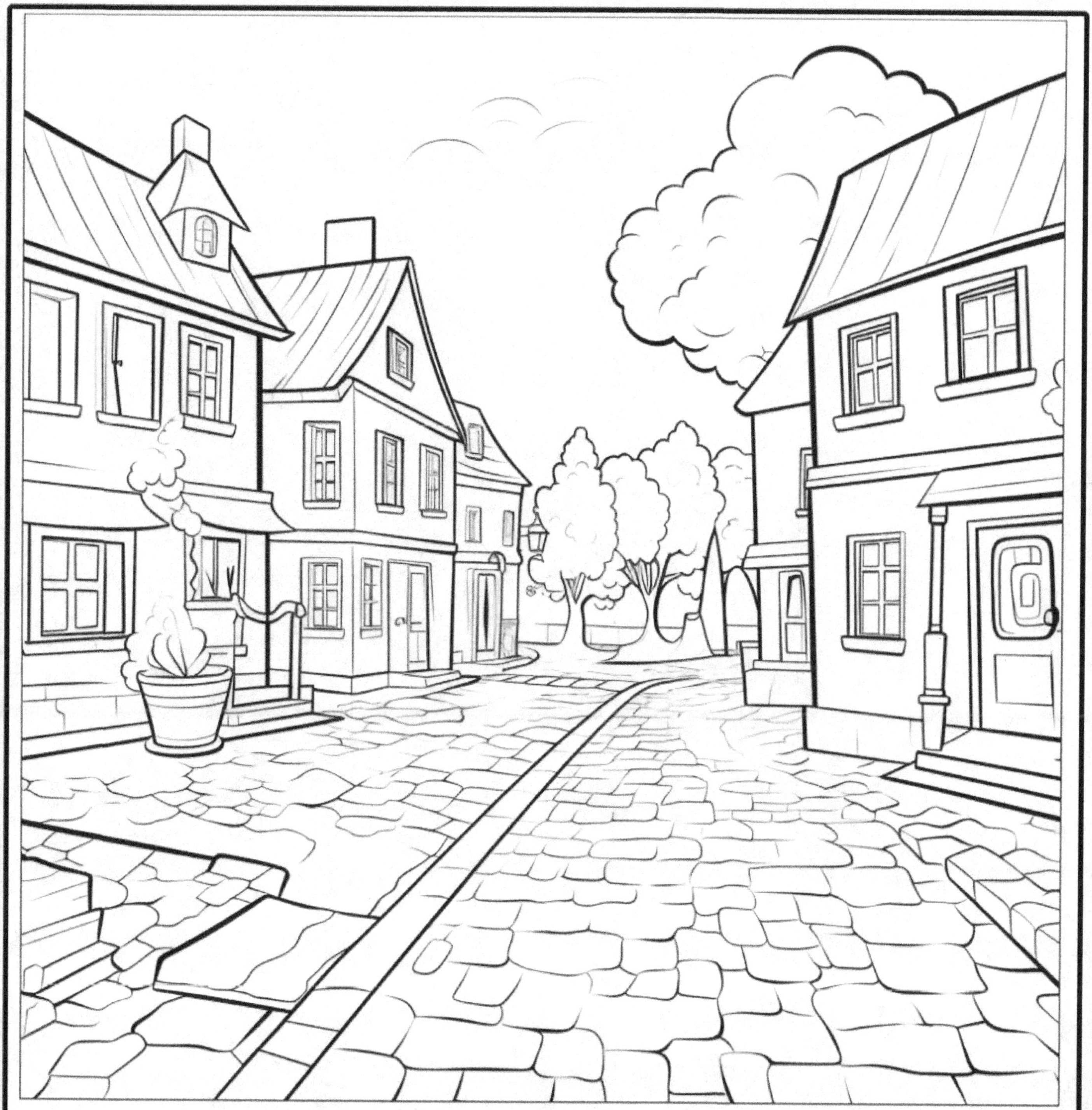

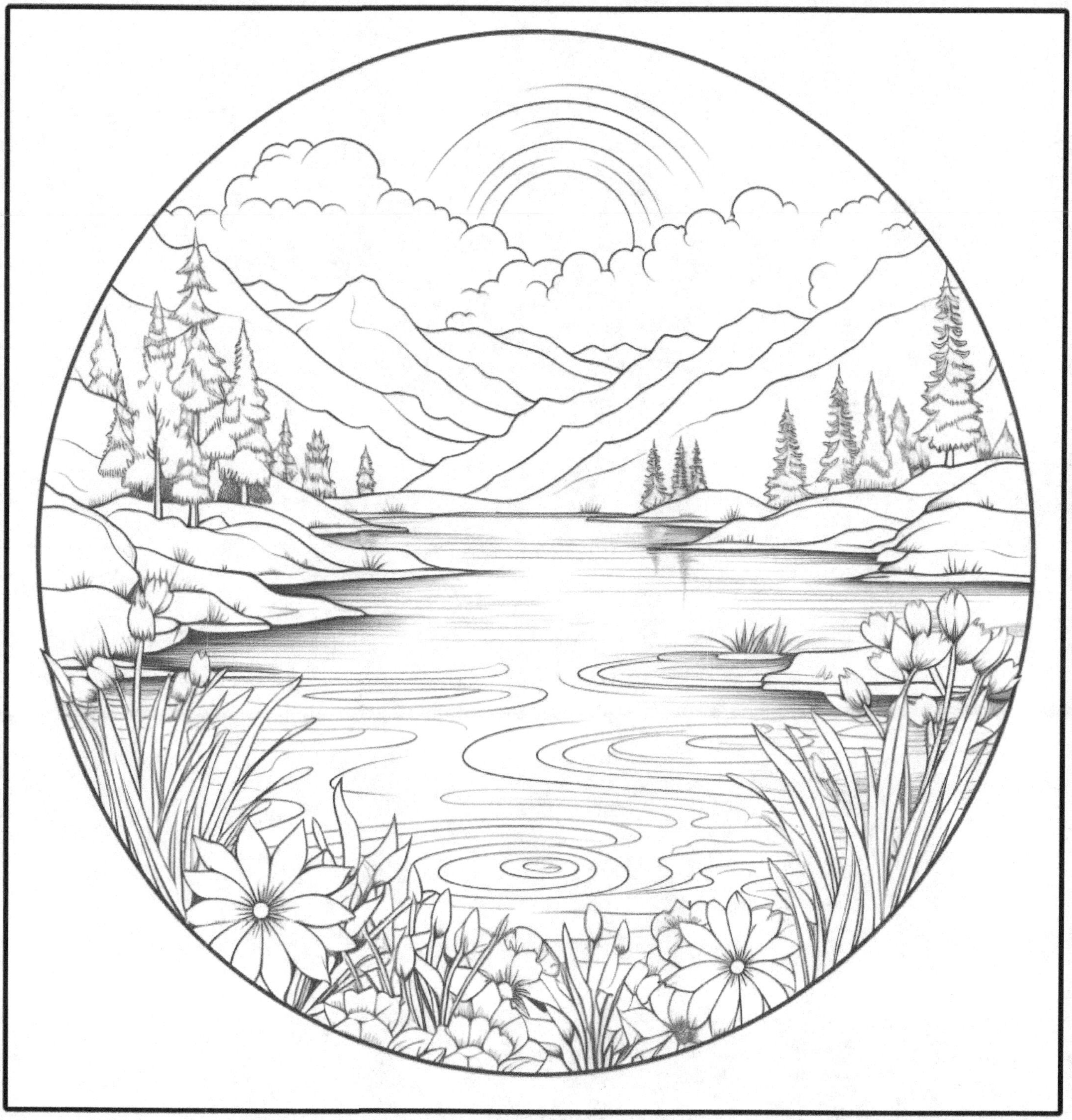

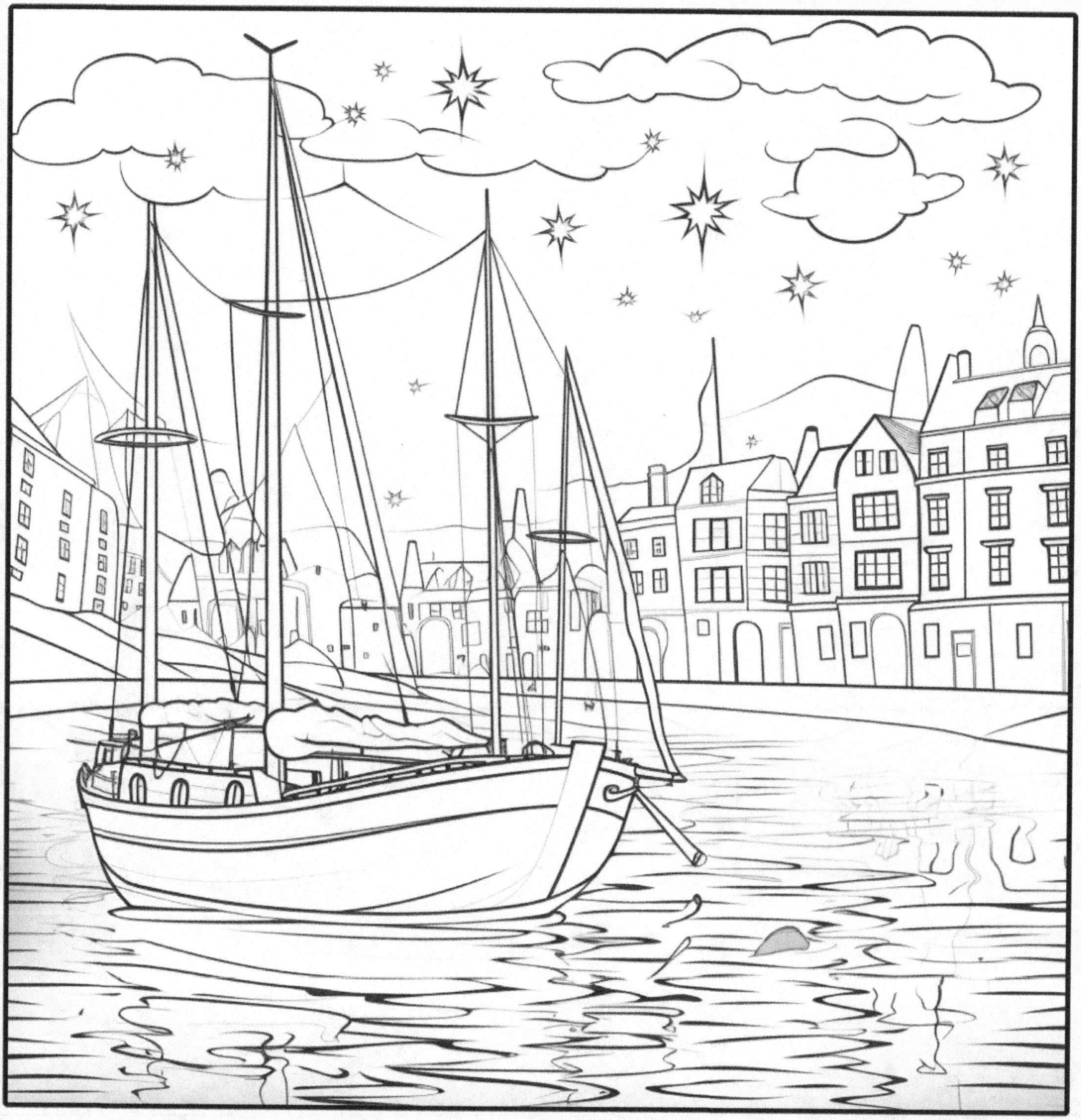

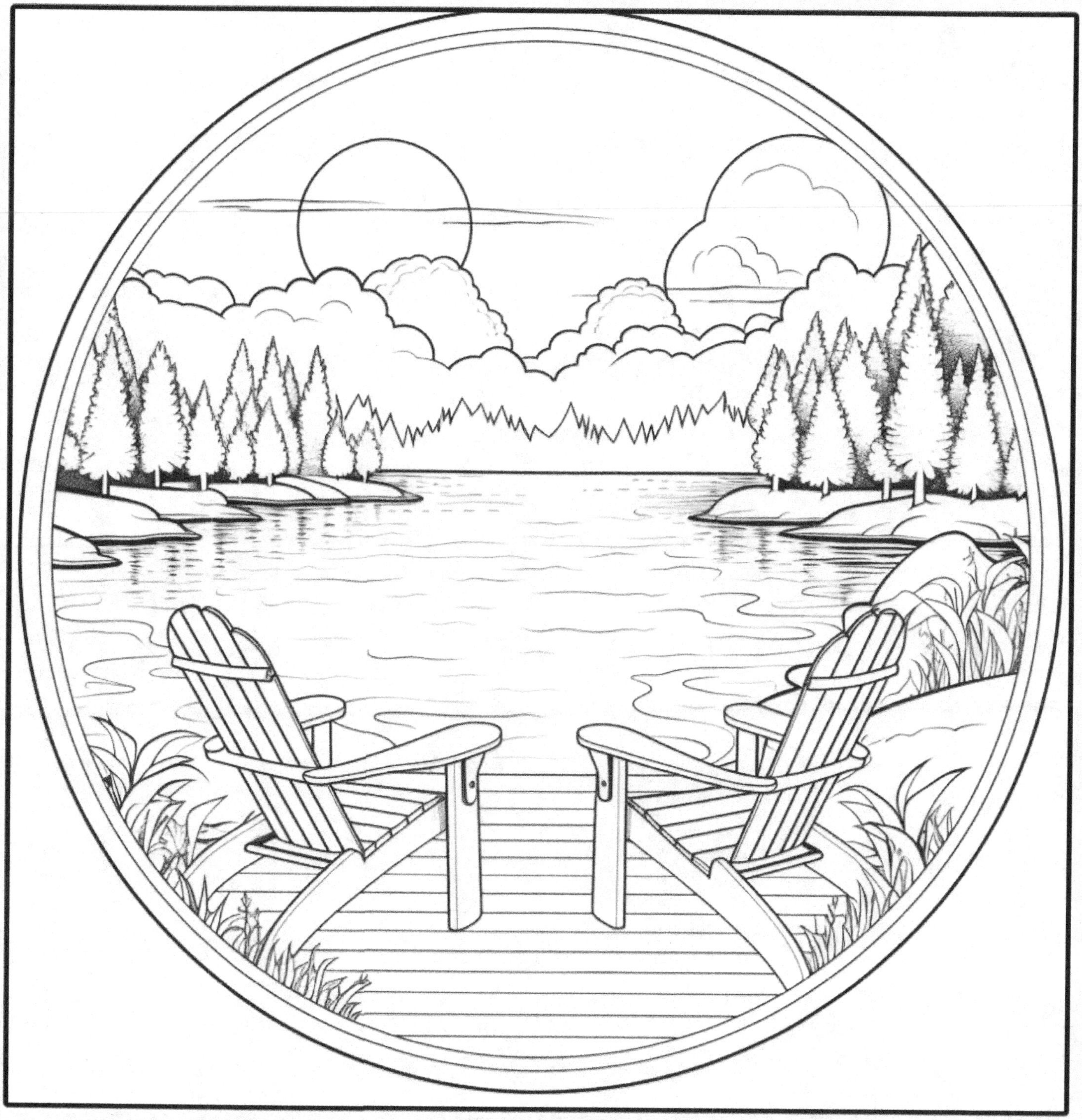

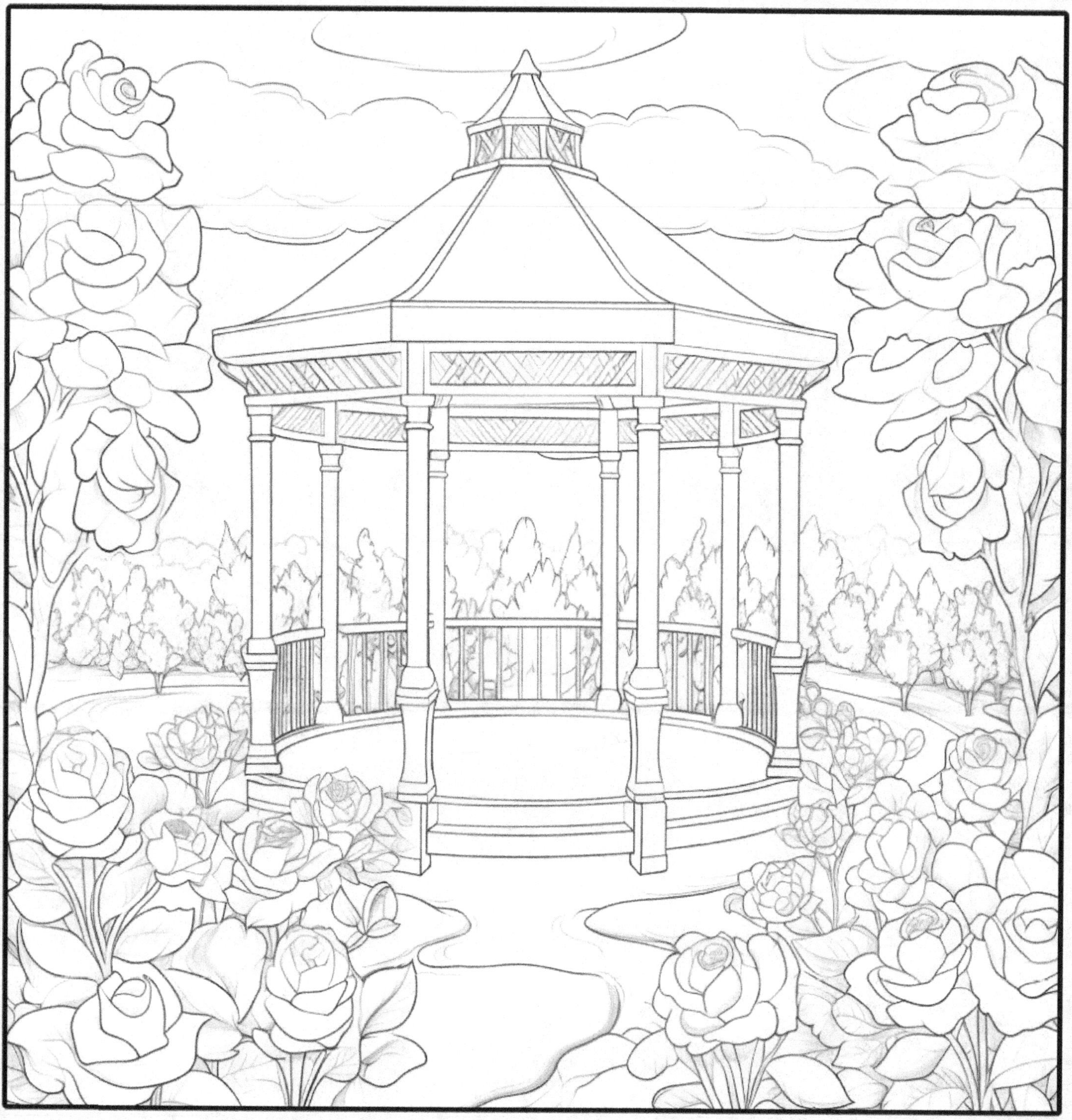

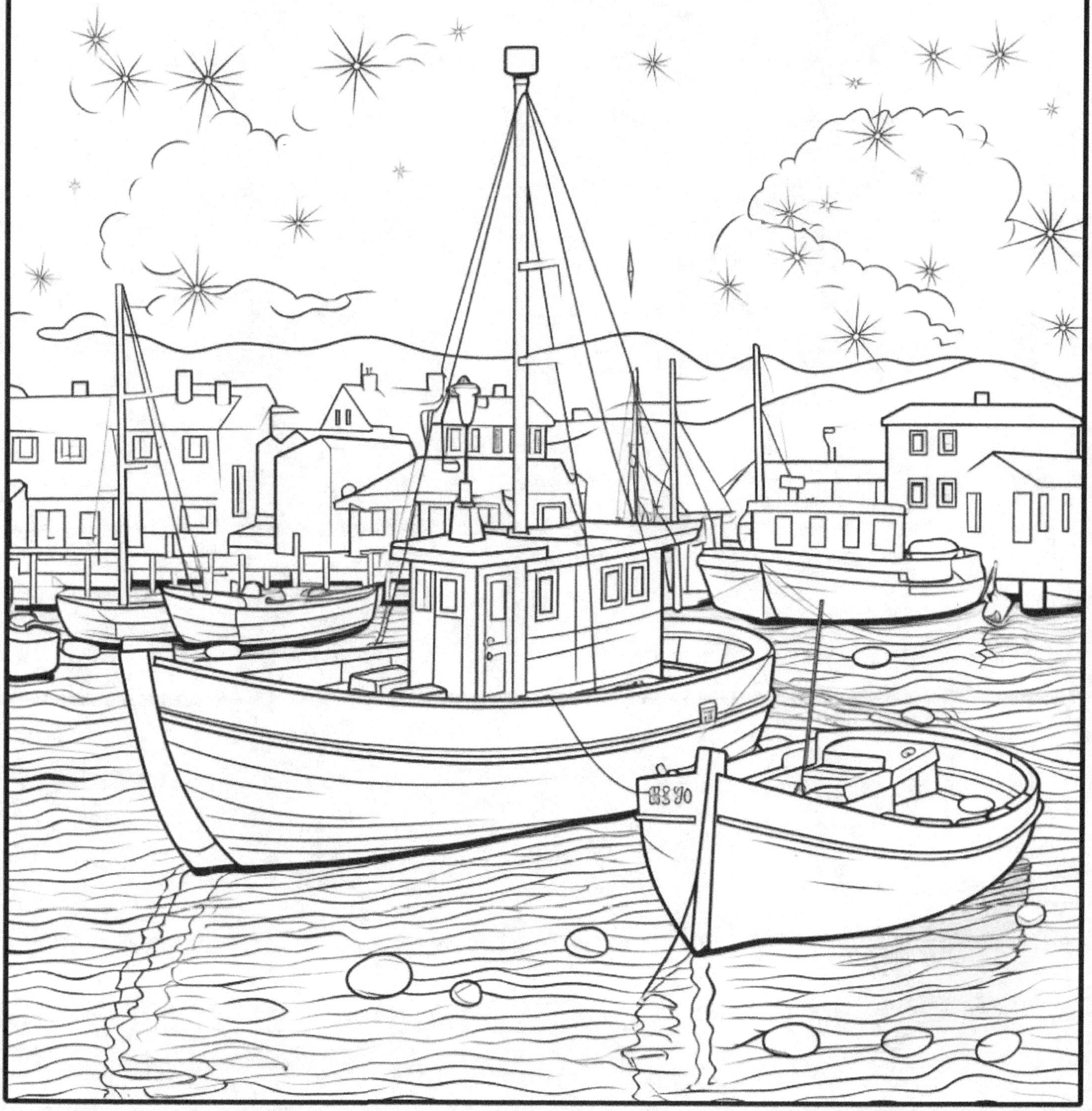

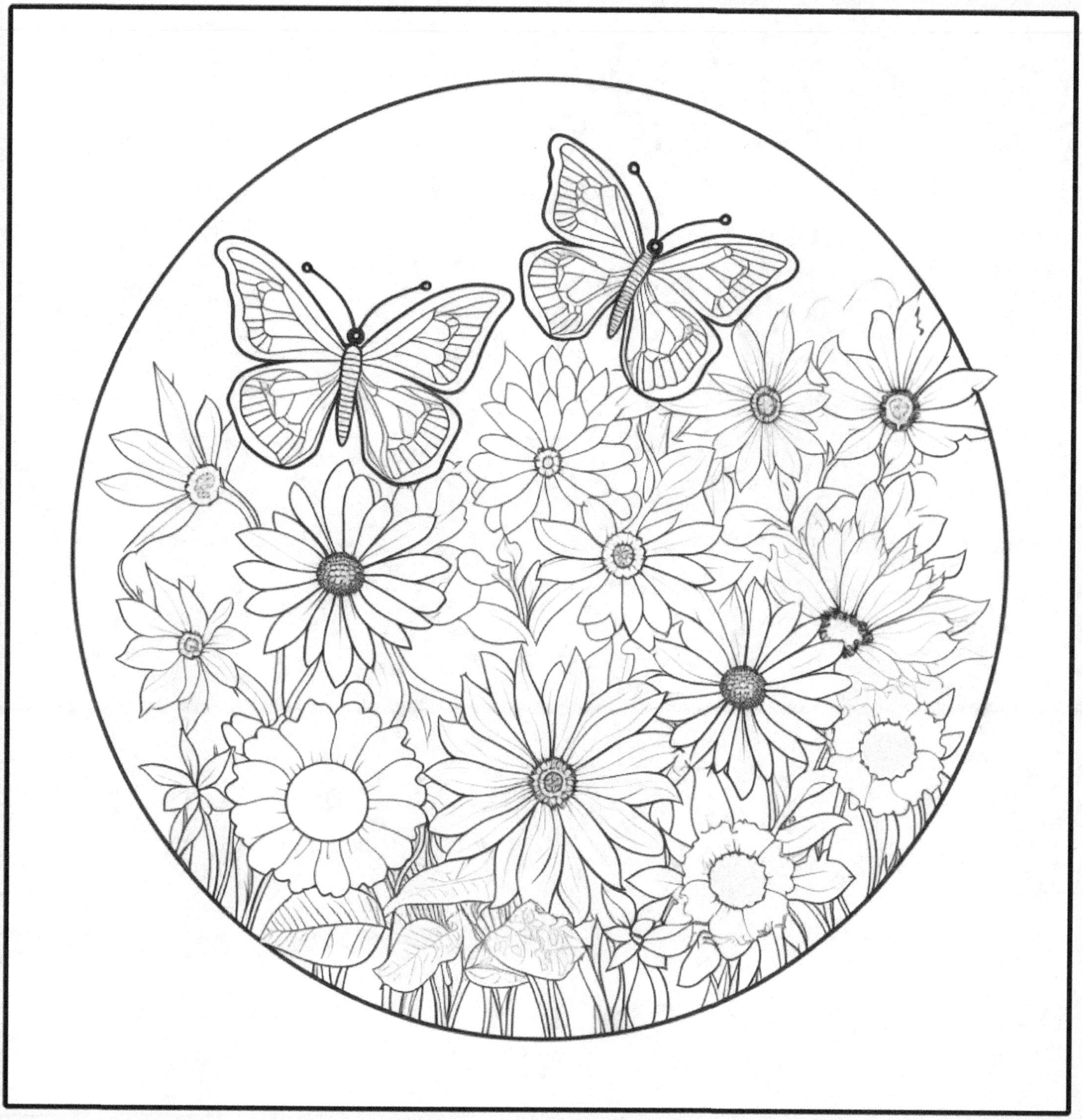

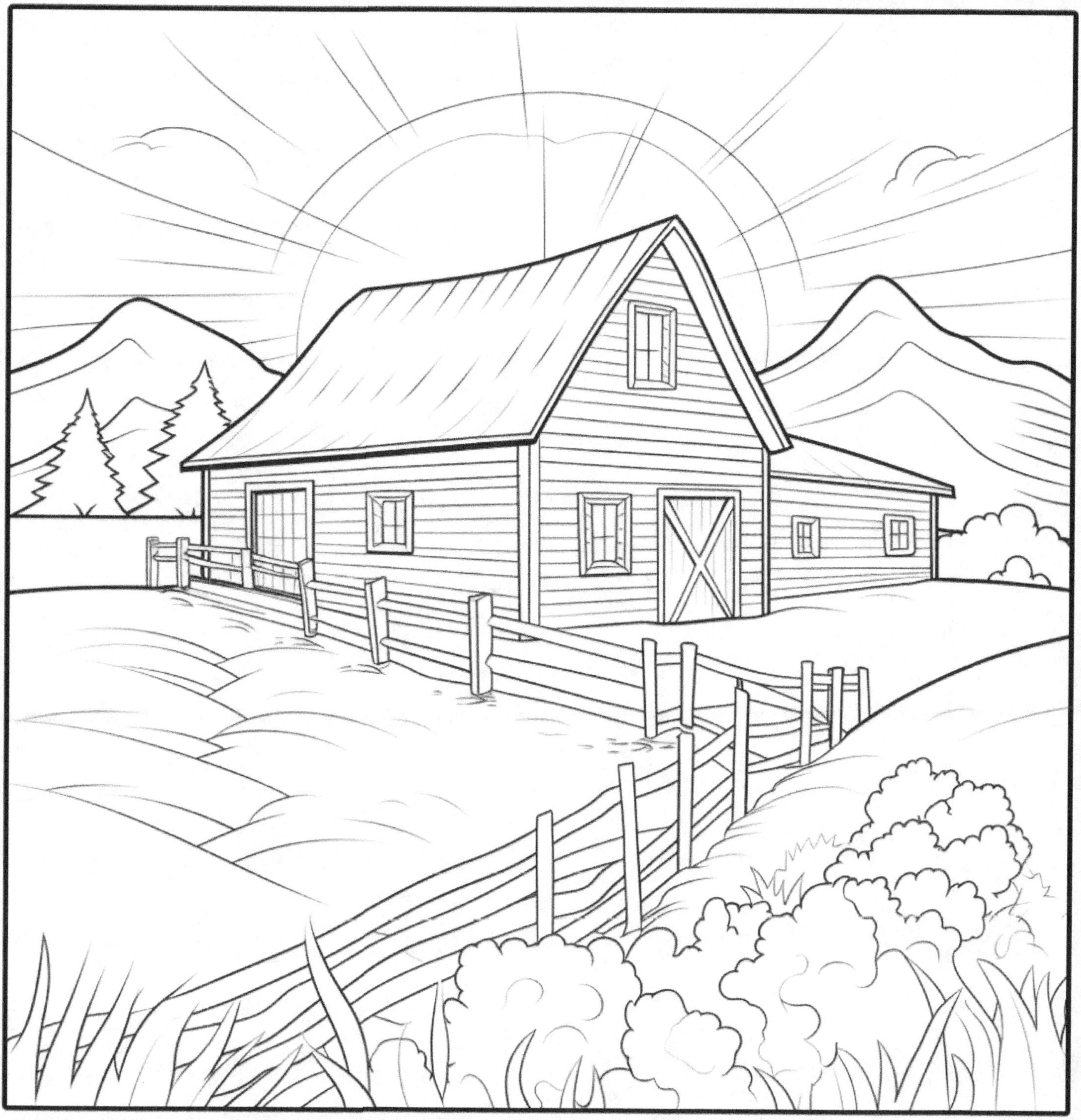

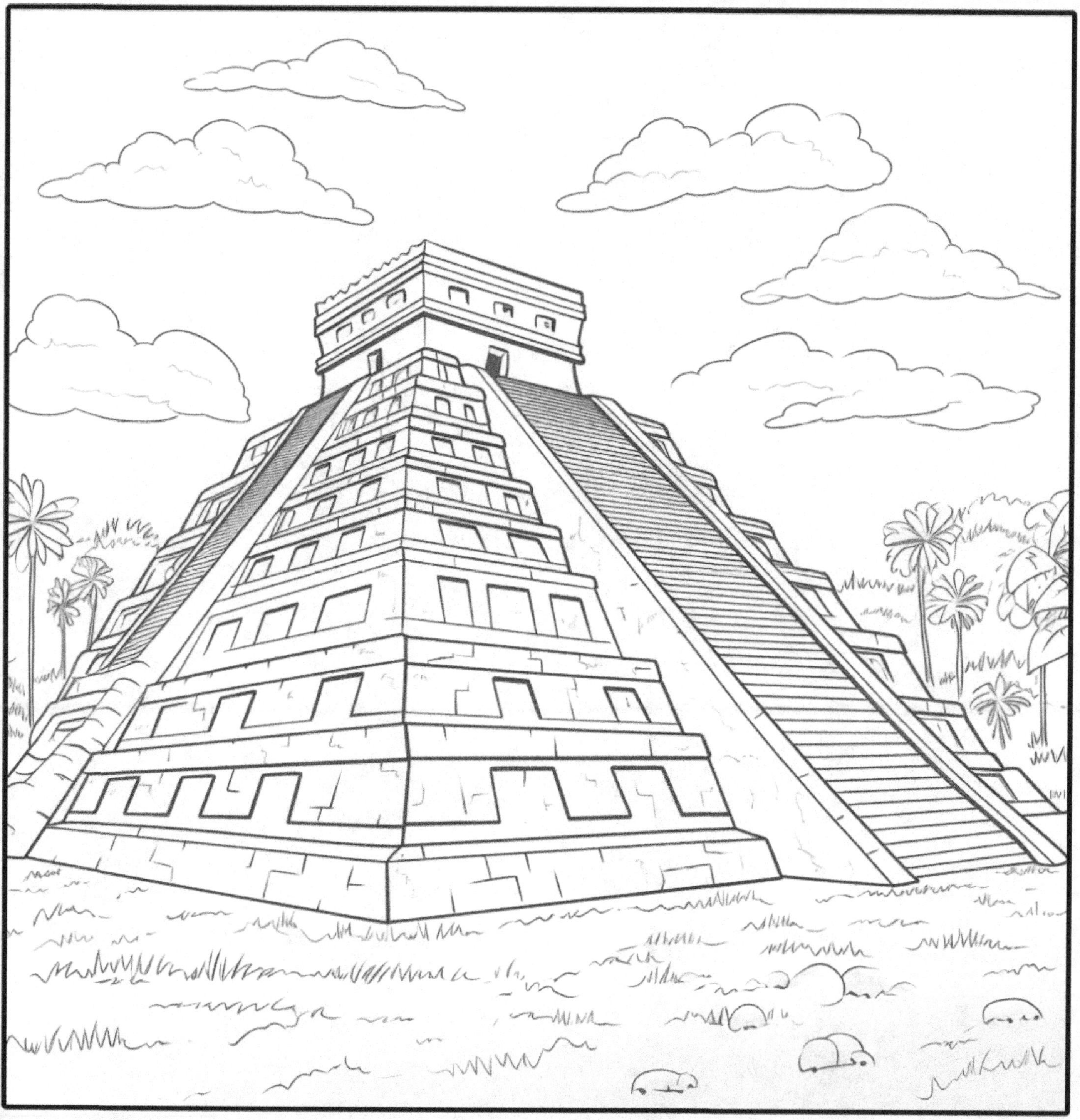

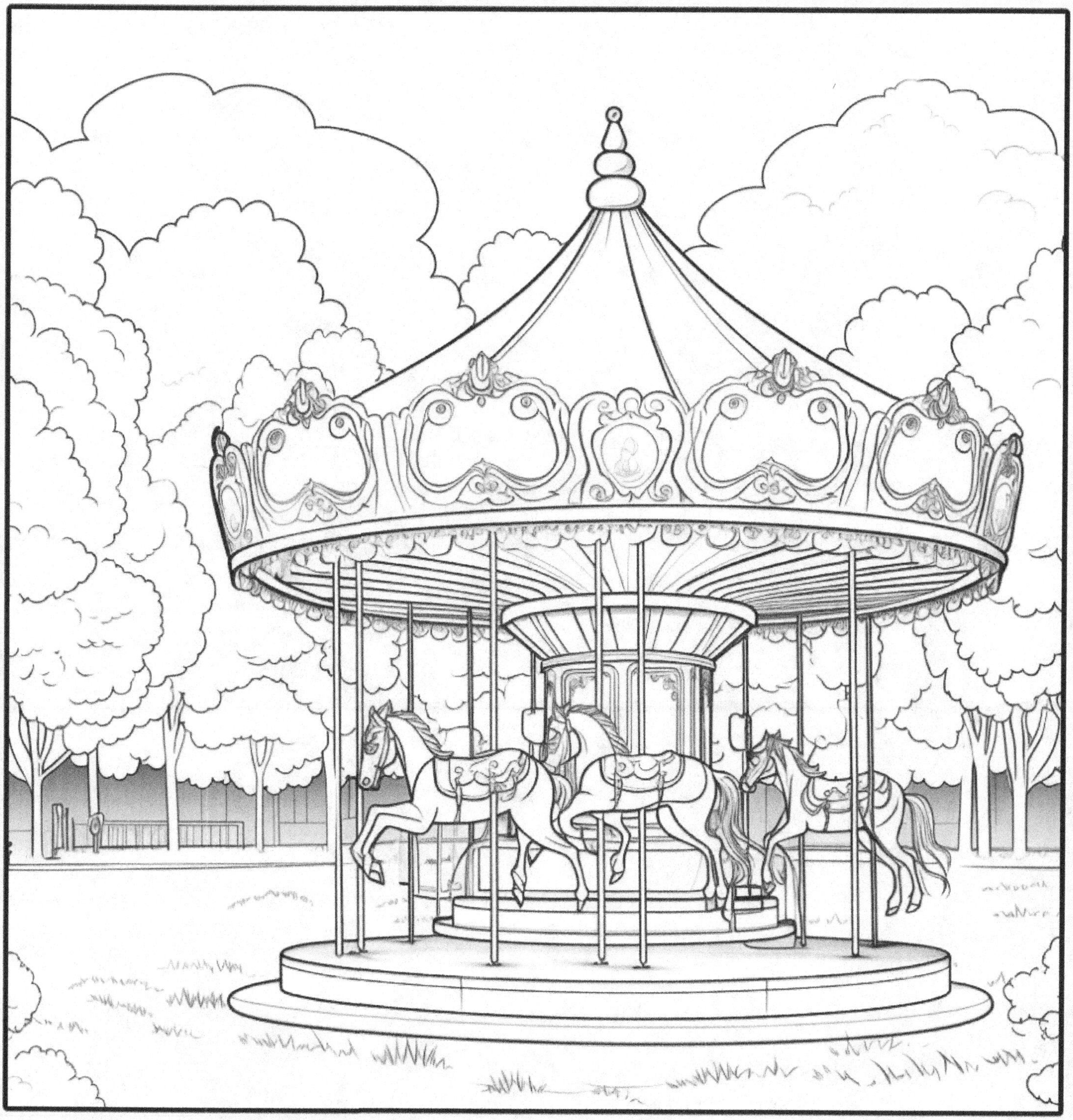

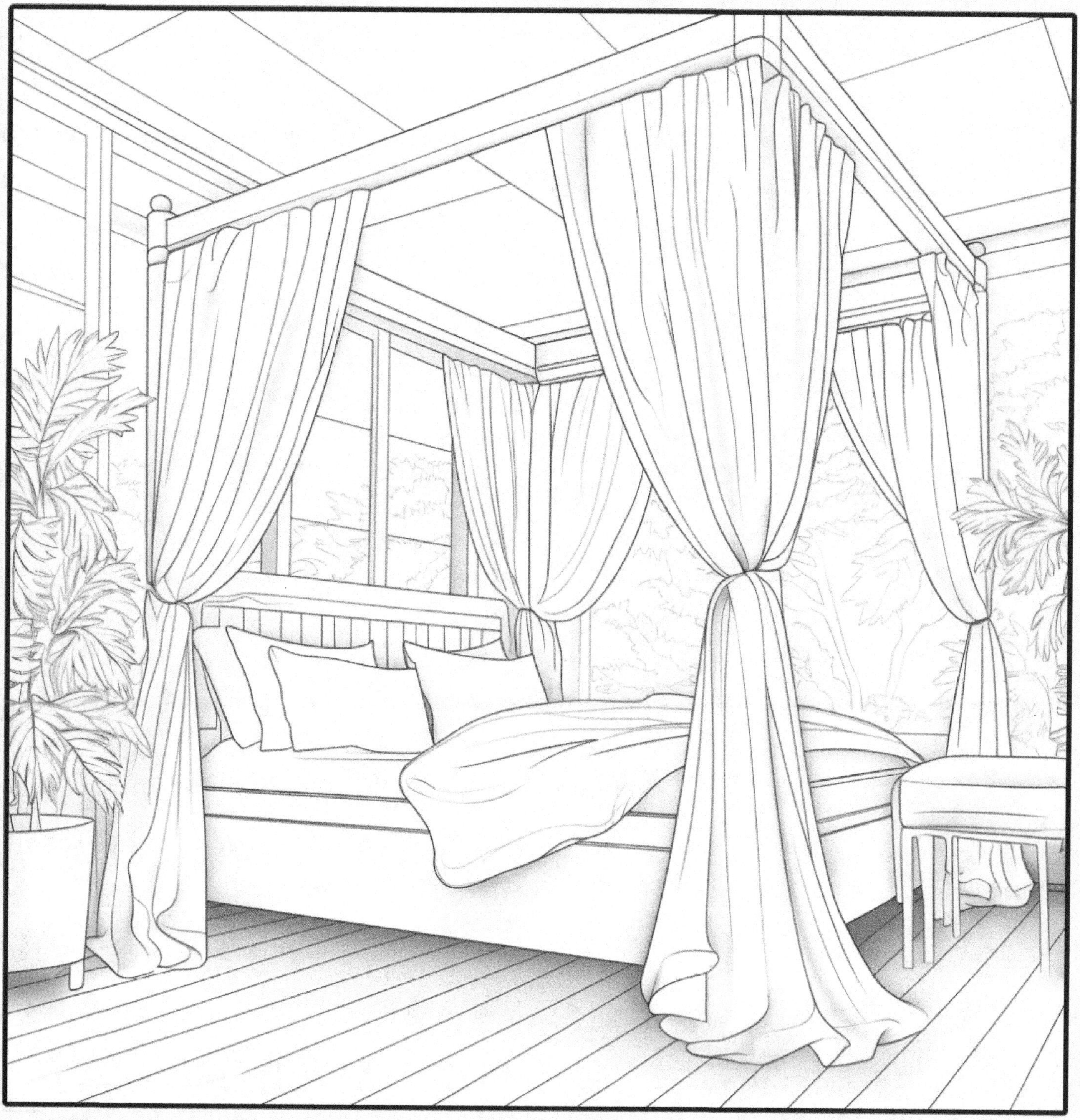

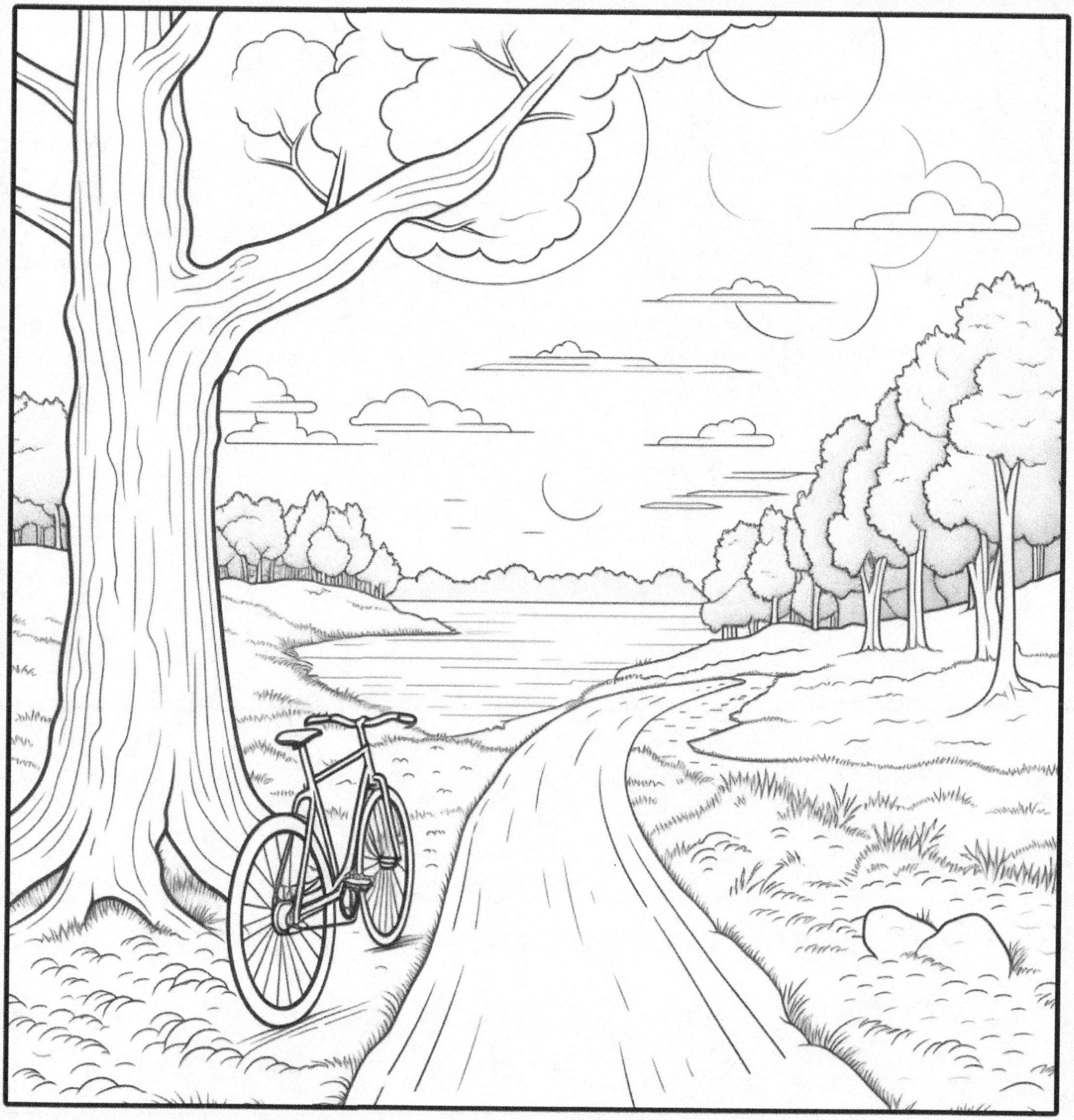

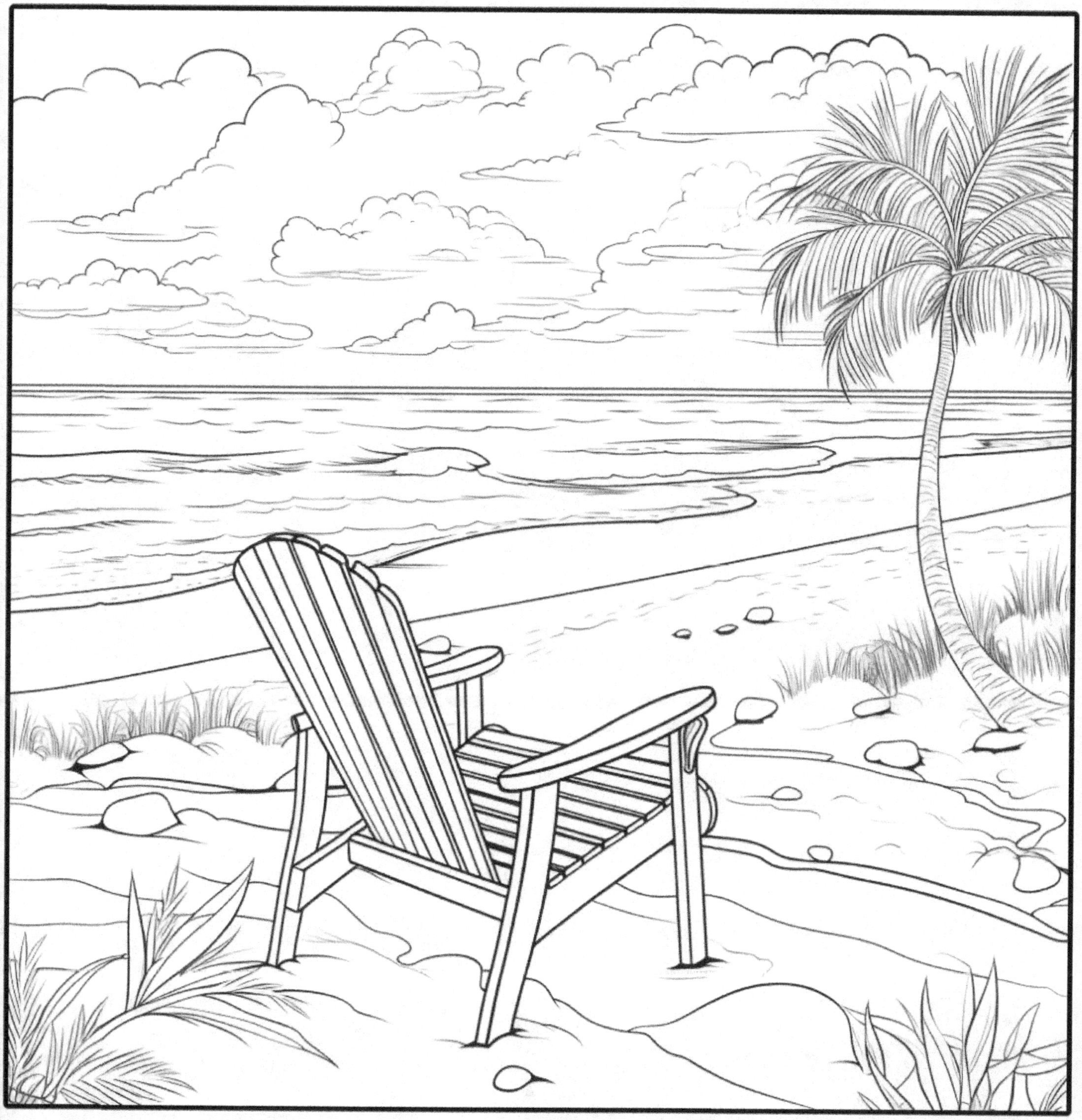

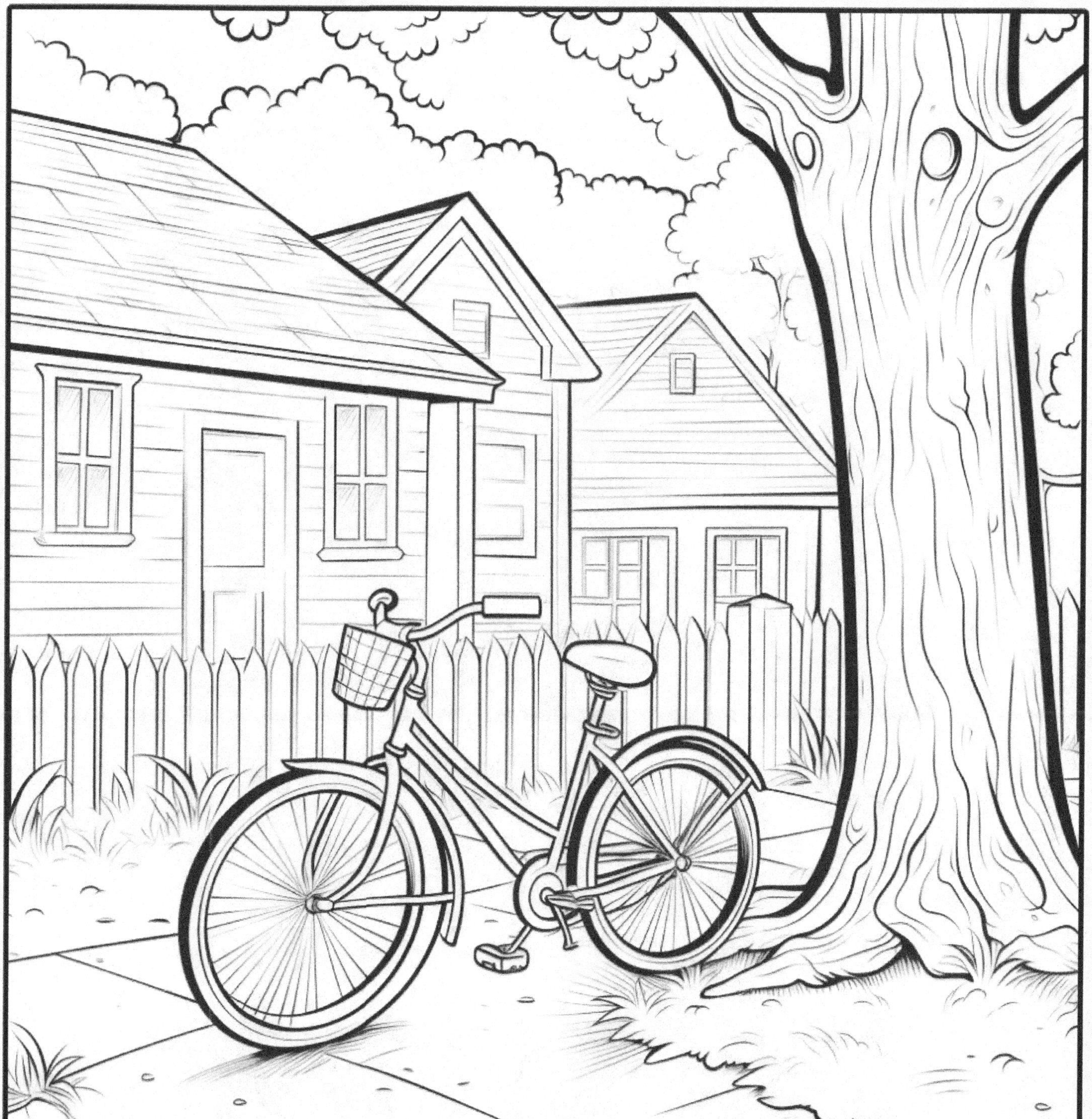

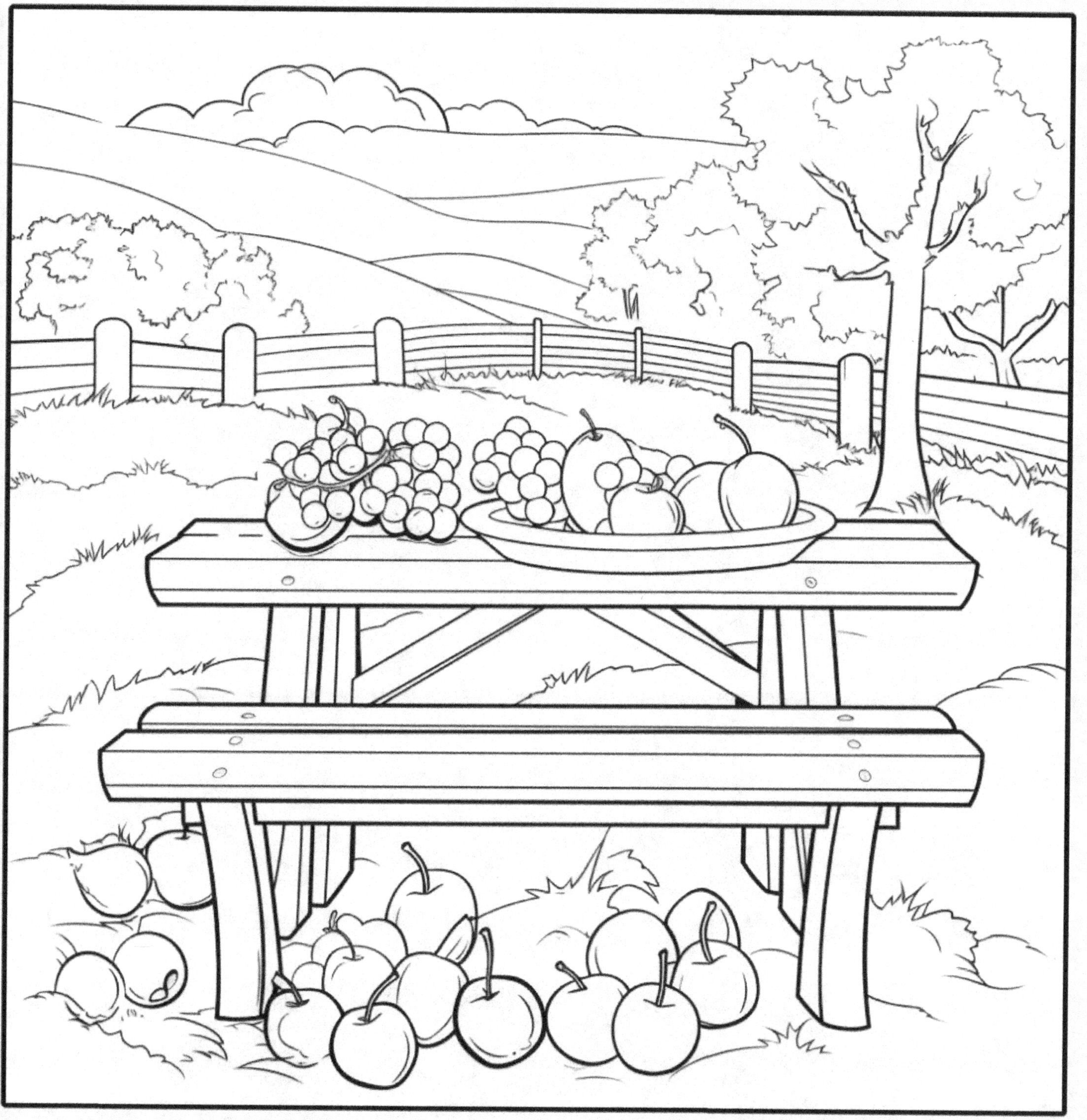

Made in the USA
Las Vegas, NV
26 October 2023

79707344R00063